ESSENTIAL SKILLS

—— FOR ——

SUCCESS

I0479421

ESSENTIAL SKILLS

—FOR—

SUCCESS

A COMPREHENSIVE GUIDE FOR TODAY'S WORKPLACE

ANDRÉ REIS, Ph.D.

CROSSOVER PRESS

Essential Skills for Success
A Comprehensive Guide for Today's Workplace

PAPERBACK ISBN: 979-8-3923-5078-0

Library of Congress Control Number: 2023906422

Name: Reis, André.
Title: Essential Skills for Success: A Comprehensive Guide for Today's Workplace/André Reis.
Description: Crossover Press, 2023 | Includes bibliographical references.
Identifiers: ISBN 979-8-3923-5078-0 (paperback)
Subjects: LCSH: Business | Management
Cover Design: André Reis; image: FreePik

DEDICATION

Lovingly dedicated to my wife

Francini

and beloved daughters

Pam, Chloe & Mckayla

Many waters cannot quench love,
rivers cannot wash it away.
If one were to give all the wealth
of his house for love,
it would be utterly scorned.

—King Solomon

CONTENTS

FOREWORD

Employers today demand a broader set of skills of employees than in times past. While technical knowledge is undoubtedly essential for excelling in any field, it is soft skills that set an individual apart and give them a competitive edge. Soft skills allow individuals to develop emotional intelligence, communicate effectively, and collaborate in a professional setting. These skills are often difficult to quantify but are vital to professional success.

In *Essential Skills for Success: A Comprehensive Guide for Today's Workplace,* André Reis, Ph.D., synthesizes concepts and practical ideas garnered from the literature to develop the skills needed to succeed in today's dynamic and complex work environment.

Divided into four parts and elegantly set with main points in bold typeface to facilitate retention, the book covers personal, interpersonal, team, and organizational skills. Each part is composed of chapters that provide a comprehensive overview of each skill, making it accessible to readers of all levels. The author has designed each chapter to be engaging, informative, and easy to understand, with practical advice that readers can easily apply in their professional careers.

Each chapter is followed by a helpful review, and each part closes with questions for discussion useful for readers looking to test their knowledge and track their progress as they work to develop their skills. These tools make this book an excellent resource for the classroom, from undergraduate to graduate level courses.

Whether you are a seasoned leader or a recent graduate starting your professional career, this book is a valuable resource for developing new skills. The wealth of resources quoted alone makes this book worth your investment.

Congratulations on taking the first step toward developing the skills needed to succeed in today's complex social and organizational systems.

Dr. Paulo Macena
Director, *The Leadership Institute*
Columbia, Maryland

INTRODUCTION

> *"Management is the art of getting things done through people."*
>
> — Peter Drucker

Management skills refer to all the knowledge and abilities necessary for the performance of any leadership or management activity. Possessing these skills is essential for professional and personal growth.

Management skills comprise different skills that leadership theories point out as essential. In this book, these skills are divided into four parts: **personal, interpersonal, team,** and **organizational.**

Personal

- Self-awareness
- Stress management

- Analytical and creative problem-solving
- Emotional intelligence

Interpersonal

- Conflict management
- Negotiation
- Assertive and effective communication
- Motivation and empathy
- Leadership

Team

- Empowerment & delegation
- Team building
- Leading positive change

Organizational

- Strategic thinking
- Organizational communication
- Communication as a business strategy

Management skills are essential for success in any organization. These skills include the ability to **communicate effectively**, make **informed decisions**, and **inspire** and **motivate** others. Effective leaders can build strong relationships with their team members, which helps to increase trust and respect and foster a sense of pride in the organization (Kouzes & Posner, 2007).

Effective communication is vital in the workplace as it comprises the ability to convey ideas and information clearly to others, as well as the ability to actively listen and respond to feedback. Effective leaders can communicate their **vision** and **goals** in a way that inspires and motivates others to work toward them. Successful managers can build strong relationships with their teams by regularly communicating with them and actively listening to their feedback and concerns. Effective communication is not just about speaking and writing but also about **understanding** and **interpreting nonverbal** cues and **adapting** communication style to the audience and context (Buckingham & Coffman, 1999).

Another critical management skill is the ability to **make informed decisions**. Effective leaders can **analyze information** and **make decisions** that are in the best interest of their organization. They can evaluate the **pros** and **cons** of different options and choose the one with the most positive impact. **Effective decision-making** also involves considering long-term consequences and potential risks and involving stakeholders in the process. Effective leaders can make decisions **quickly and effectively**, even under pressure, and can explain their reasoning clearly and logically (Kouzes & Posner, 2007; Northouse, 2016).

Inspiring and motivating others is another key leadership skill (Buckingham & Coffman, 1999). Effective managers can create a **positive** and **energetic work environment** where team members feel valued and motivated to do their best. They can provide clear **direc-**

tion and *guidance* while allowing team members to think creatively and take initiative. Effective leaders can also recognize and reward their team's accomplishments, which helps to **build morale** and foster a **sense of pride** in the organization. Inspiration and motivation can also be achieved by creating a **culture of learning**, growth, and development and providing opportunities for feedback and recognition (Bass, 1990).

Effective leaders also possess a high level of **emotional intelligence,** the *ability to* **recognize, understand,** *and* **manage** *one's emotions and those of others.* Emotionally intelligent leaders can **empathize** with their team members, understand their needs, and respond appropriately. The strong relationships they develop with team members help to increase **trust** and **respect** in the workplace. Such leaders can handle conflicts and difficult situations calmly and professionally. E.I. also involves **self-awareness, self-regulation, self-motivation,** and using emotions to facilitate thinking and social interactions (Goleman, 2006; Salovey & Mayer, 1990).

Successful leaders are also capable of **adapting to change** (Kouzes & Posner, 2007). They can anticipate and respond to changes in the business environment, both internal and external. They **identify new opportunities** and leverage them while navigating difficult situations. Such leaders **inspire** and **motivate** members to adapt to change, which helps to create a culture of innovation and growth. Adaptability also involves being **resilient, flexible,** and **open-minded** to learning and improving (Gardner & Avolio, 1998).

In addition to the above-mentioned management skills, effective leaders must be proficient in **strategic thinking.** Strategic thinking involves the ability to think beyond the present and envision a future that is aligned with the organization's goals and objectives (Mintzberg, 1994). Leaders who possess this skill can *analyze market trends, anticipate potential challenges, and identify opportunities to innovate and grow the organization.* They can also develop and implement **long-term plans** and **strategies** that help the organization achieve its goals and objectives. In today's constantly changing business environment, strategic thinking is increasingly important for organizational success (Hitt, Ireland, & Hoskisson, 2017).

Another essential skill for effective leadership is **coaching** and **mentoring**. Coaching and mentoring involve *guiding and supporting team members to help them develop their skills and reach their full potential* (Whitmore, 2017). Leaders who master this skill can *identify the **strengths** and **weaknesses*** of their team members and provide them with the necessary feedback and guidance to help them improve their performance. They can also offer their team members the necessary **training** and **development opportunities** to enhance their skills and capabilities. Coaching and mentoring not only help to improve the performance of team members but also help to build a strong and loyal team that is committed to the organization's goals and objectives (Luthans & Peterson, 2002).

Finally, successful leaders understand and employ the power of **innovation and creativity**. These skills consist of the ability to think outside the box, generate new ideas, and find novel solutions to problems (Amabile, 1988). Leaders who possess this skill can create a **culture of innovation** within the organization and encourage their team members to think creatively and come up with new ideas. They can also **leverage technology** and other resources to drive innovation and create a **competitive advantage** for the organization. Innovation and creativity are becoming increasingly important in today's fast-paced business environment, where organizations must constantly adapt and evolve to remain competitive (Christensen, 1997).

In conclusion, effective leadership requires a **diverse set of management skills** that include *personal*, *interpersonal*, and *team* skills. These skills include *effective communication, decision-making, motivation and empathy, emotional intelligence, adaptability, strategic thinking, coaching and mentoring, and innovation and creativity.*

Leaders who possess these skills can build **strong relationships** with their team members, create a **positive work environment,** and **drive organizational success.** Organizations must facilitate a workplace where these skills can be developed in their leaders, fostering organizational competitiveness.

Review

1. Managerial skills are all the knowledge and capabilities necessary for the performance of any management and leadership activity.

2. Managerial skills encompass different types of skills that leadership theories point out as essential for a manager.

3. Interpersonal managerial skills include conflict management, negotiation, assertive and effective communication, motivation and empathy, and leadership.

4. Innovation and creativity involve the ability to think outside the box, generate new ideas, and find novel solutions to problems.

5. Emotional intelligence (E.I.) refers to the ability to recognize, understand, and manage one's own emotions and the emotions of others.

6. Effective leaders can create a positive and energetic work environment where team members feel valued and motivated to do their best work.

PART I
PERSONAL
MANAGEMENT SKILLS

CHAPTER 1

SELF-AWARENESS

> *"The better you know yourself, the better your relationship with the rest of the world."*
>
> — Toni Collette

It has been demonstrated that **self-awareness** is an essential skill for managers because it *enables them to work from emotional self-regulation and self-motivation as the central axis for intrapersonal understanding.* Self-awareness also develops interpersonal relationships, where **motivation**, **empathy**, the development of **social skills**, **persuasion**, and **influence** stand out as critical factors.

Self-awareness is the *process of understanding one's own abilities,*

11

values, personality, and motivations. Developing self-awareness is essential for personal growth and effective decision-making both in personal and professional contexts. Self-awareness allows people to understand their **strengths** and **weaknesses**, establish realistic goals, and make informed decisions. Studies have shown that identifying one's unique strengths, perspectives, and experiences generates **novel ideas** and **solutions** (Hu, Liden, & Wu, 2011).

According to the *self-determination theory*, self-awareness is an essential aspect of **autonomous motivation,** which is linked to better health and psychological well-being. Self-aware individuals identify and understand their own values, making decisions that align with their beliefs and personal goals (Deci & Ryan, 2000).

There are several ways to develop self-awareness. One way is through **self-reflection,** which involves taking the time to reflect on one's own thoughts and actions. This can include writing a journal, meditating, or engaging in therapy. Another way to develop self-awareness is through **self-assessment,** which can consist of taking personality tests or assessments, such as the Myers-Briggs Type Indicator or the Five-Factor Model (Costa & McCrae, 1992). Additionally, **feedback from others** can be valuable for developing self-awareness, as it can provide a different perspective on oneself (Riggio, 2009; Boyd & Myers, 2011).

The benefits of having a solid sense of self-awareness are numerous. Firstly, people with a strong sense of self-awareness are more likely to be **self-confident** and **assertive**, leading to better communication and decision-making. Additionally, self-awareness can lead to better **emotional regulation**, as people can better understand and manage their emotions. Finally, self-awareness can lead to **better relationships**, as people can better understand and communicate their needs and values to others (Furnham, 2006).

One of the essential benefits of self-awareness is its ability to increase **self-esteem** and **resilience.** When individuals have a strong sense of self-awareness, they are better equipped to handle criticism and negative feedback from others. They are also better able to recognize their strengths and accomplishments, which helps boost their self-confidence. Furthermore, self-awareness enables individuals to learn from their **failures** and **setbacks,** contributing to their overall resilience and ability to overcome challenges (Brown & Ryan, 2003).

Another crucial aspect of self-awareness is its impact on leadership. Self-aware leaders can understand their strengths and weaknesses, which enables them to **delegate tasks effectively** and surround themselves with individuals who complement their skills (Day, Fleenor, Atwater, Sturm, & McKee, 2014). Self-awareness also helps leaders **communicate** more effectively with their team members, as they are more **empathetic** and can tailor their communication style to suit different personalities and preferences (Boyatzis, Smith, & Blaize, 2006).

Additionally, self-awareness plays a vital role in personal **development** and **growth**. By understanding their own values, motivations, and personality, individuals can make informed decisions that align with their goals and aspirations. Self-awareness also enables individuals to identify areas for improvement, which can help them **set realistic goals** and work toward **self-improvement** (Lam, 2017).

Self-awareness also plays a key role in enhancing **creativity** and **innovation**. Self-aware individuals are also more **open to diverse viewpoints** and **feedback**, which can lead to more innovative outcomes. Therefore, developing self-awareness can not only **enhance personal growth** but also foster a culture of innovation within organizations (Amabile, 1998).

Another relevant aspect is the relationship between self-awareness and **job satisfaction**. Research demonstrates that self-aware individuals are more satisfied with their jobs and report higher levels of job performance (Barrick & Mount, 1991). Self-awareness helps individuals **align their values** and strengths with their job **responsibilities**, leading to a greater sense of **purpose** and **fulfillment** (Sosik & Megerian, 2014). Organizations can benefit from promoting self-awareness among their employees, improving job satisfaction and performance.

Self-awareness enables individuals to reflect on their ethical values and beliefs, leading to more **ethical decision-making** (Tenbrunsel & Smith-Crowe, 2008). By understanding their biases and motivations, individuals can **avoid unethical practices** and make decisions that align with their moral principles (Kerns & Barclay, 2011). Therefore, promoting self-awareness can contribute to building a culture of **ethical leadership** and **decision-making** within organizations.

In conclusion, self-awareness is a critical skill that enables individuals to *develop a deeper understanding of themselves and their abilities*. As such, it is essential for **personal growth**, **effective decision-making,** and **leadership**. A strong sense of self-awareness boosts self-confidence, emotional regulation, and better interpersonal relationships.

Self-awareness can be developed through self-reflection, self-assessment, and input from others. By embracing self-awareness, individuals can reap the numerous benefits it provides, such as improved decision-making and a more fulfilling life.

Review

1. Self-awareness allows one to understand his or her own abilities, values, personality, and motivations.

2. Self-awareness enables individuals to reflect on their ethical values and beliefs, leading to more ethical decision-making

3. Self-reflection is a way to develop self-awareness, which involves reflecting on one's thoughts and actions.

4. Input from others can be valuable for developing self-awareness because it provides a different perspective on oneself.

5. Having a strong sense of self-awareness leads to better emotional regulation and interpersonal relationships.

6. Self-awareness also plays an important role in enhancing creativity and innovation.

> *"The greatest weapon against stress is our ability to choose one thought over another."*
>
> — William James

CHAPTER 2

STRESS MANAGEMENT

Stress is a common experience that affects people of all ages and backgrounds. It is the *physiological and psychological response to perceived threats or challenges* (APA, 2017). Stress can have negative consequences on an individual's **physical** and **mental health**, leading to a variety of health problems, including **cardiovascular disease**, **diabetes**, and **depression**. Stress management is an important aspect of maintaining overall health and well-being (Kroenke, Spitzer, & Williams, 2007).

17

One of the most effective ways to control stress is through **regular physical activity**, which has been shown to reduce symptoms of stress and anxiety. Exercise can also improve **mood** and overall **well-being**. Additionally, exercise **distracts from stressful factors** and provide a sense of accomplishment and control. Note that **exercise intensity** does not need to be high to be effective. Even low-intensity activities like **walking** can reduce stress levels.

Exercise is an effective stress management technique due to its ability to **reduce cortisol levels**, the stress hormone, and **improve mood**. Regular physical activity can also **increase endorphins**, the body's natural mood boosters. Exercise is also an effective method for reducing symptoms of **depression** and **anxiety**. Another effective stress management technique is **relaxation**, such as **meditation** and **deep breathing**, which effectively reduce stress levels (Kendall, 2010).

Sleep is essential for maintaining physical and mental health, and **lack of sleep** can **increase stress levels**. Studies have shown that individuals who get enough sleep have **lower cortisol levels** and are better able to cope with stress. Additionally, lack of sleep has been associated with an increased risk of developing **mood disorders** such as **anxiety** and **depression**. Therefore, individuals must prioritize getting enough sleep as a stress management technique (Chattu et al., 2020).

Social support is another important stress management technique, which includes talking to **friends** and **family** or participating in **support groups**. Studies have found that *having a strong social* *support system can have a positive impact on mental health and well-being.* Additionally, social support can provide people with a **sense of belonging** and **connection**, which can help reduce stress levels (Kendall, 2010).

Cognitive-Behavioral Therapy (CBT), a form of therapy that focuses on *changing negative thought patterns and behaviors,* is another effective technique for stress management. CBT seeks to help individuals *identify and challenge their erroneous beliefs and replace them with more realistic and positive thoughts.* Additionally, individuals are taught coping strategies for dealing with stressful situations more healthily (Beck, 2011; DiTomasso, 2011).

Lastly, **time management** is an important stress management technique. Time management is the process of *planning and organizing one's time to achieve specific goals.* Studies have found that individuals who can effectively manage their time are less likely to experience stress-related symptoms (Kendall, 2010). Additionally, effective time management can help reduce the **feeling of overwhelm**, which can be a significant source of stress.

By incorporating the techniques above into daily routines, individuals can effectively control stress levels and improve overall health and well-being:

1. **Set priorities.** Decide which tasks must be done and which can wait, and learn to say no to new tasks if you are overwhelmed.

2. ***Stay in touch with people who can provide emotional and other support.*** Seek help from friends, family, and community or religious organizations to reduce stress related to work responsibilities or family issues, such as caring for a loved one.

3. ***Take time to engage in relaxing activities*** you enjoy, such as reading, doing yoga, or gardening.

4. ***Avoid obsessively thinking about problems.*** Focus on what you have accomplished, not what you have been unable to do.

5. ***Exercise regularly.*** A moderate walk of just 30 minutes a day can help lift your mood and reduce stress.

If you feel that you can't cope with stress or have suicidal thoughts, seek help from a mental health professional. In conclusion, **stress** is a common experience that affects people of all ages and backgrounds. Stress can have negative consequences on an individual's physical and mental health, leading to a variety of health problems. There are several different stress management techniques that can be used to reduce stress levels, such as exercise, relaxation, social support, cognitive-behavioral therapy, and time management. Stress management is an important aspect of maintaining overall health and well-being.

Review

1. Stress is the physiological and psychological response to challenges or threats.

2. Exercise is an effective way to control stress due to its ability to reduce cortisol levels, the stress hormone.

3. Relaxation techniques, such as meditation and deep breathing, are effective in reducing stress levels.

4. Social support is another important stress management technique that can give people with a sense of belonging and connection.

5. Cognitive-Behavioral Therapy (CBT) is a form of therapy that focuses on changing negative thought and behavior patterns.

6. Time management is an important stress management technique. Time management is the process of planning and organizing one's time to achieve specific goals.

7. Sleep is essential for maintaining physical and mental health, and lack of sleep can lead to increased stress levels.

CHAPTER 3

ANALYTICAL AND CREATIVE PROBLEM-SOLVING

> *"The significant problems we face cannot be solved at the same level of thinking we were at when we created them."*
>
> — Albert Einstein

Analytical problem-solving is a process that *involves using different approaches and skills to solve a problem or overcome a challenge*, while **creative problem-solving** *focuses on generating an original solution.*

Most people find it difficult to solve problems creatively. However, both analytical and creative problem-solving processes are fundamental to success in any field, whether it be in business, academia, or personal life. The problem-solving process begins with **identifying the problem**,

23

followed by generating **possible solutions** and **evaluating** and **selecting** the best option.

Analytical problem-solving is based on the *ability to analyze and break down a problem into its fundamental components and use logic and reason to find a solution.* This may involve using **statistical** and **mathematical tools** or considering factors such as feasibility, cost, and associated risks with each option. Analytical problem-solving also *involves a careful evaluation of available data and information.*

Creative problem-solving refers to the *ability to generate new ideas and unconventional approaches to solve a problem.* It involves **thinking outside the box** and considering **non-obvious** options and **unique perspectives**, which may include using **imagination** and **intuition**, as well as exploring different perspectives and combining seemingly unrelated concepts. Creativity can be developed through practice and learning techniques such as **lateral thinking** and **brainstorming**.

Each approach comes with caveats. A purely creative approach can generate **non-viable** or **unrealistic ideas**, while a strictly analytical approach can lead to the selection of **safe** but **uncreative** options. Therefore, it is important to find a balance between creativity and analysis when solving problems. In many cases, the optimal solution to a problem *involves a combination of both creative and analytical approaches.*

For example, in the field of advertising, a creative strategy may be necessary to **grab the attention** of the audience and generate interest in a product or service, while an analytical approach is essential to **measure the impact** of the campaign and adjust it accordingly.

Creative and analytical problem-solving is essential in the business world, as companies often face complex and changing challenges that require a combination of unconventional thinking and rigorous data analysis to solve. Companies must be able to adapt quickly to changes and find new opportunities. This requires a *combination of creativity to generate new ideas and analysis to evaluate the viability of those ideas*. For example, a company may use a creative approach to **develop new products** or **services** while also using an analytical approach to evaluate the **financial feasibility** of such products or services.

In the field of technology, creative and analytical problem-solving is essential for the development of new products and services. For example, software developers must be able to think creatively to design **innovative solutions** while also being able to analyze and solve **complex technical problems**. In academia, students must be able to apply their knowledge and skills to solve complex problems in a variety of disciplines. This requires the **ability to think critically** and **analytically**, as well as the ability to **generate new ideas** and **approaches** (Cropley, 2006).

In conclusion, *both analytical and creative problem-solving are essential skills for success in various fields*. While analytical problem-solving involves breaking down a problem and using logic and reason to find a solution, creative problem-solving consists of generating original ideas and approaches.

However, a **balance** between the two approaches is crucial for **optimal problem-solving**; a strictly creative approach may generate non-viable ideas, while erring on the side of analytical problem-solving may lead to uncreative outcomes.

The ability to adapt and find new opportunities in the face of changing challenges requires a combination of both approaches. Therefore, it is essential to develop both analytical and creative problem-solving skills to tackle complex challenges in various fields.

Review

1. Analytical problem-solving is a process that involves the use of different approaches and skills to solve a problem or overcome a challenge, while creative problem-solving focuses on generating an original solution.

2. The problem-solving process begins with identifying the problem, followed by generating possible solutions and evaluating and selecting the best option.

3. The analytical solution is based on the ability to analyze and break down a problem into its fundamental components and use logic and reason to find a solution.

4. Creative problem-solving refers to the ability to generate new and unconventional ideas and approaches to solve a problem.

5. A purely creative approach may generate non-viable or unrealistic ideas, while a purely analytical approach may lead to the selection of safe but uncreative options.

CHAPTER 4

EMOTIONAL INTELLIGENCE

> "Emotional intelligence is not the opposite of intelligence, it is not the triumph of heart over head; it is the unique intersection of both."
>
> — Daniel Goleman

Emotional Intelligence (E.I.) refers to the *ability to understand and adequately manage our own emotions and those of others* (Goleman, 1998). According to Salovey & Mayer (1990), it refers to the *ability to recognize and understand our own emotions and the emotions of others and to use this information to guide thinking and behavior*. It is an important skill to have healthy and successful relationships at work and in personal life.

The concept of E.I. was first introduced by psychologist ***Daniel Gole-***

man in the late 1990s. Goleman proposed that E.I. comprises four key components: *self-awareness, self-regulation, social awareness,* and *social skills.*

Self-awareness refers to the ability to understand and recognize our emotions and how they influence behavior.

Self-regulation refers to the ability to manage and control our own emotions and reactions.

Social awareness refers to the ability to understand and recognize the emotions of others, and **social skills** refer to the ability to use this understanding to build relationships and communicate effectively (Goleman, Boyatzis, and McKee, 2002).

E.I. is a **strong predictor of success** in the workplace. A study by Goleman, Boyatzis, and McKee (2002) found that E.I. is a better **predictor of success** in leadership roles than cognitive intelligence or technical skills. Similarly, a study by Lopes, Côté, and Miners (2006) found that E.I. is a significant **predictor of job performance** in a sample of employees from various industries. The following are some critical points about E.I.:

1. *E.I. is not the same as cognitive intelligence or Intelligence Quotient* (IQ), which refers to the ability to process information and reason (Gardner, 1983). However, E.I. and cognitive intelligence are related and can influence each other.

2. *E.I. can be developed and improved* through conscious practice and reflection.

3. *E.I. is vital for having healthy and successful relationships at work and in my personal life.* For example, people with higher E.I. tend to be more effective in communication and conflict resolution and also tend to be more capable of motivating and leading others (Salovey & Mayer, 1990).

4. *E.I. can also be necessary for our mental and physical health.* People with higher E.I. tend to be more resistant to stress and are less likely to develop mental disorders such as anxiety and depression.

5. *E.I. has an impact on our happiness and well-being.* People with higher E.I. tend to be more capable of managing negative emotions and finding joy and meaning in life (Bar-On, 1997).

E.I. is a *critical component of effective leadership and management in the workplace.* One of the key advantages of having a high level of E.I. in the workplace is the ability to have **positive relationships** with colleagues. Individuals with high E.I. can *understand the emotions of others and respond appropriately* (Goleman, 1998), allowing them to build relationships of trust and respect with colleagues, improving communication and collaboration in the workplace.

In addition to these benefits, E.I. also plays a role in **stress management** and well-being in the workplace (Carmeli & Josman, 2008). Individuals with high E.I. can recognize and understand their own emotions in **stressful situations**, which allows them to effectively manage stress. People with high E.I. can **better handle stress**, which makes them better performer and **more resilient to challenges**. This allows them to maintain their emotional balance and make clear and rational decisions in pressure situations. They are also more likely to be satisfied with their jobs and have a positive attitude toward work (Lopes et al., 2004).

One of the key ways in which E.I. contributes to success in the workplace is by **improving communication** and **teamwork**. They can also **handle conflicts** and **negotiate mutually beneficial solutions.**

E.I. also plays a critical role in **decision-making** and **problem-solving** that benefits the organization and employees. People with high E.I. *consider the emotional implications of their decisions and take a more holistic approach to problem-solving*. This allows them to create **win-win solutions** in difficult situations. Emotionally intelligent individuals can **empathize with others**, allowing them to make decisions that take into account the needs and concerns of all stakeholders (Goleman, 1998; Salovey & Mayer, 1990; Bar-On, 1997).

Some studies have found that women score higher than men on emotional expressiveness and empathy, which are components of social awareness. Other studies have suggested that **cultural differences** can affect the expression and recognition of emotions, with some cultures valuing emotional restraint and others valuing emotional expressiveness (Fischer & Manstead, 2000; Schutte, Malouff, Thorsteinsson, Bhullar, & Rooke, 2007; Matsumoto, Yoo, & Fontaine, 2008).

Therefore, it is crucial to consider these factors when developing E.I. in the workplace. *Organizations should recognize the potential impact of cultural and gender differences on the development and manifestation of E.I. and tailor their training programs and coaching strategies accordingly.* For instance, training programs can include modules on cultural sensitivity and diversity, which can help employees develop **cross-cultural communication skills** and increase their awareness of cultural differences in emotional expression and recognition.

E.I. is not always easy to develop. Many people struggle with one or more of the components of E.I. However, various strategies can be used to develop E.I. in the workplace. Some of the most effective strategies are **training, coaching**, and **mentoring**. Many organizations offer training programs that teach people to recognize and understand emotions, manage their feelings, and communicate effectively with others (Lopes et al., 2004).

In conclusion, E.I. is essential in the workplace as it allows for **positive relationships** with colleagues, **handling stress**, and effective **decision-making**. Organizations need to foster E.I. to create a productive, collaborative work environment (Goleman, 2001; 2002).

Individuals should also strive to develop their own E.I., as this will allow them to be successful not only in their careers but also in their personal life. With **conscious practice** and **reflection**, E.I. can be developed and improved (Salovey & Mayer, 1990).

Review

1. Emotional intelligence is the ability to understand and manage our own emotions and those of others.

2. The concept of E.I. was introduced by psychologist Daniel Goleman in the late 1990s.

3. E.I. is composed of four key components: self-awareness, self-regulation, social awareness, and social skills.

4. E.I. has been shown to be a strong predictor of success in the workplace and is important for having healthy and successful relationships at work and in personal life.

5. E.I. is vital for mental and physical health, happiness, and well-being.

6. According to Salovey & Mayer (1990), E.I. refers to the ability to recognize and understand one's own emotions and the emotions of others and use this information to guide thought and behavior.

CHAPTER 5

POSITIVITY

> *"Positive thinking will let you do everything better than negative thinking will."*
>
> — Zig Ziglar

Research suggests that **positivity** leads to **success** in the workplace.[1] Contrary to common belief, **happiness** leads to success rather than the other way around. Positive employees exhibit better decision-making, creativity, productivity, resilience, and interpersonal skills, giving companies a competitive advantage.

Positivity refers to the *frequent experience of positive emotions like joy, hope, gratitude, serenity, and*

---

1 This chapter is based on Elizabeth Cabrera, "The six essentials of workplace positivity," *People & Strategy 35/1* (2012), 50–60.

inspiration. Positive emotions at work correlate with *higher levels of engagement, organizational citizenship behavior,* job **performance**, and lower likelihood of burnout or counterproductive behavior. Positivity not only benefits the bottom line but also enhances **employee well-being** and personal **success.** Organizations that prioritize employee well-being and foster positivity can gain **loyalty** and **commitment** from their employees.

There are six essentials of workplace positivity: positive *thinking, positive relationships, strengths, empowerment, meaning, and well-being.* Each dimension is accompanied by specific steps to increase positivity. By utilizing this framework, managers and human resource professionals can enhance **employee engagement** and **performance**, ultimately achieving greater organizational success. For instance, happy college students were found to have **higher earnings** 15 years after graduation, and employees who reported being the happiest received **better supervisor evaluations** and **pay increases** 18 months later.

Positivity brings a wide range of benefits to individuals, contributing to their success. **Mentally,** positive emotions broaden our **focus** and **mindset**, allowing us to consider a greater **range of ideas** and **solutions**. Positive individuals are **more mindful** and **open** to information, leading to **better decision-making** and **increased creativity.** Feeling safe and secure, they can think divergently without feeling threatened. Doctors who are in positive mood were **quicker** and **more creative** in diagnosing a complex case when compared to those in a neutral mood. Additionally, managers with higher positivity levels make **more accurate decisions** and are more effective leaders.

Positive emotions have several **social, psychological,** and **health benefits.** Socially, positive individuals have **stronger relationships, cooperate** more readily, and are more likely to help others (Lyubomirsky, King & Diener, 2005). In the workplace, having high-quality relationships is related to **personal growth, creativity,** and **motivation**. Additionally, positive emotions lead to better judgments of others and increased liking, which strengthens relationships (Clifton & Nelson, 1992).

Psychologically, positivity **enhances cognitive** and **interpersonal skills**, builds psychological resources, and increases motivation. Positive individuals experience **less anxiety, lower levels of depression,** and have higher levels of hope, self-confidence, and resilience. They are more motivated to set **higher goals,** generate multiple pathways to reach their goals, and bounce back from setbacks (Lyubomirsky, King & Diener, 2005).

Health-wise, positive people have **lower blood pressure, heart rates,** and levels of stress-related hormones. They also have *stronger immune systems, better sleep, fewer colds, and experience less pain.* Additionally, positive people may **live up to 10 years longer** than negative people due to the many health benefits of positivity (Danner, Snowdon & Friesen, 2001).

To increase positivity, individuals can focus on their own **thoughts and actions,** which account for 40 percent of their positivity. While **genetics** determine about 50 percentof happiness and life circumstances only account for 10 percent, individuals can **intentionally raise their happiness** set point through effort. However, humans have a **negativity bias,** reacting more strongly to negative events and remembering them more (Hanson, 2009). It is crucial to have a *three-to-one ratio of positive-to-negative emotions to counterbalance the negativity bias* (Fredrickson, 2009).

In the workplace, managers can create positive environments by implementing **policies and practices** that encourage positive **thinking** and **behavior** (Pearson & Porath, 2009). This can lead to increased **employee engagement, effectiveness,** and **productivity,** giving companies a **competitive advantage** (Pearson & Porath, 2009).

Research in positive psychology has identified numerous interventions that have been proven to increase positivity. Cabrera (2012) developed a framework for workplace positivity and identified **strategies** that can be implemented by managers in order to create and maintain positive workplaces where people thrive (Achor & Peterson, 2008; Diener & Seligman, 2002; Dutton, 2003; Harter, Schmidt & Hayes, 2002).

The **Six Essentials of Workplace Positivity** are: *positive thinking, positive relationships, strengths, mpowerment, meaning, well-being.* Each is explored below.

Positive Thinking. The way we think has a powerful effect on our emotions and behavior, and abilities. *People who engage in positive thinking before an intelligence test perform better compared to those who think negatively* (Achor & Peterson, 2008). While we often can't control what happens to us, we can control how we think about it. Managers can help create a positive work environment by encouraging positive thinking.

Four strategies for promoting positive thinking include positive **focus, optimism, gratitude,** and **forgiveness** (Achor, 2010; Seligman, 2002).

1. Positive focus involves *intentionally focusing on what is good and ignoring small negative annoyances* (Achor, 2010). Managers can remain focused on the positive by directing conversations toward what is going well, celebrating small wins, pointing out strengths, telling success stories, and encouraging teams to search for solutions (Sanders, 2011).

2. Optimism is *expecting a desirable future and believing that goals can be accomplished*. Optimistic individuals see **setbacks as temporary** circumstances they can overcome, while pessimistic individuals view setbacks as longer-lasting situations they cannot control. Managers can help people **dispute pessimistic thoughts** and develop a more optimistic explanation of negative situations (Seligman, 2002).

3. Gratitude involves being thankful and appreciating the good things in life. Managers should encourage employees to cultivate gratitude through practices such as keeping a gratitude journal or starting meetings by expressing gratitude (Brown et al., 2003).

4. Forgiveness is an essential aspect of positivity as dwelling on negative experiences decreases positivity. Managers can foster a culture of forgiveness by encouraging employees to forgive one another and by modeling forgiveness themselves (Achor & Peterson, 2008).

Positive relationships are vital for well-being and effectiveness in the workplace (Diener & Seligman, 2002; Dutton, 2003). Four key strategies for building positive relationships include **respect and appreciation, recognition, trust,** and **generosity** (Dutton, 2003; Rath & Clifton, 2005).

1. Respect and appreciation are foundational for positive relationships. Managers can demonstrate respect and appreciation by **actively listening** to employees, involving them in decision-making, and valuing their opinions (Dutton, 2003).

2. Recognition plays a crucial role in building positive relationships. It shows employees that their **contributions are valued** and that their **work matters.** Managers should provide day-to-day and above-and-beyond recognition for employees' accomplishments (Rath & Clifton, 2005).

3. Trust is essential for positive relationships, and managers can build trust by acting with integrity, consistency, and benevolence. Managers should also demonstrate trust in their employees by giving them autonomy and sharing valuable information (Dutton, 2003).

4. Generosity, including acts of giving and helping others, contributes to workplace positivity. Managers can encourage generosity by recognizing and appreciating acts of kindness and by creating opportunities for employees to support and help one another (Sanders, 2011).

Recognizing and leveraging individual **strengths** is a key component of workplace positivity (Harter et al., 2002). When individuals are able to use their strengths in their work, they experience **higher levels of engagement, satisfaction,** and **productivity**. Managers can facilitate the identification and utilization of strengths through the following strategies:

1. Strengths assessment: Encourage employees to **identify** their personal strengths through assessments such as the VIA Character Strengths survey. This self-awareness helps individuals understand their unique qualities and how they can contribute effectively (Peterson & Seligman, 2004).

2. Strengths-based assignments: Assign tasks and projects that align with employees' strengths, allowing them to utilize and develop their core abilities. Managers should provide opportunities for employees to excel in areas where they naturally thrive.

3. Strengths recognition: Acknowledge and appreciate employees' strengths and their contributions resulting from those strengths. Managers should **provide feedback** that highlights the specific strengths demonstrated by individuals, recognizing their positive impact on the team and organization.

Empowering employees involves providing them with the autonomy, resources, and support they need to perform their roles effectively (Spreitzer, 1995). Empowered employees feel a sense of **control over their work,** which enhances their motivation and well-being.

The following strategies can help managers foster empowerment:

1. Autonomy: Grant employees a certain level of **independence** and decision-making authority in their work. Allow them to *have a say in setting goals, determining methods, and making decisions whenever possible.*

2. Skill development: Provide opportunities for employees to **develop new skills** and expand their knowledge. Offer training programs, workshops, and mentoring to enhance their capabilities and confidence.

3. Supportive environment: Create a supportive work culture where employees feel **safe** to express their **ideas**, voice **concerns,** and **seek assistance.** Managers should be approachable, open to feedback, and responsive to employee needs.

Many people seek **fulfillment** in their work by finding a **sense of purpose** and meaning. Cascio (2003) found that Americans value **meaningful work** more than other factors such as promotions, income, job security, and work-life balance.

Individuals perceive their work as a **job,** a **career,** or a **calling** (Wrzesniewski et al., 1997). Those who view their work as a calling find it personally meaningful and beneficial to others. Work that is **meaningful** and aligned with **personal values** and goals has a profound impact on employee well-being and satisfaction (Steger et al., 2012; Ulrich & Ulrich, 2010).

Effective leaders foster a sense of meaning by:

1. Purpose alignment: Help employees connect their work to a **broader organizational purpose** or **mission**. Clearly communicate the significance of their contributions and how they positively impact others at work or society as a whole (Ulrich & Ulrich, 2010; Grant, 2008).

2. Goal clarity: Set clear and meaningful goals that align with employees' individual aspirations and the organization's objectives. Ensure that employees understand how their goals contribute to the overall vision. Companies like Novo Nordisk facilitate interactions between employees and customers to increase awareness of the positive difference their work makes (Mainiero & Sullivan, 2006).

3 Supportive culture & social responsibility. According to Sisodia, Wolf, and Sheth (2007), individuals find a profound sense of purpose when they hold the belief that the organization they are employed by contributes to **improving the world**. Corporate social responsibility initiatives demonstrate a company's **commitment beyond profit** maximization and contribute to **employee commitment and morale.** Create a culture that values and celebrates meaningful work. Encourage employees to share stories of how their work has made a difference and recognize the positive impact they have on others (Bhattacharya, Sen & Korschun, 2008).

Leaders play a crucial role in creating positive work environments by demonstrating **genuine concern** for **employee well-being**. *Well-being* encompasses health, happiness, and prosperity (Cascio, 2003), and promoting employee well-being is crucial for fostering a positive workplace environment (Achor & Peterson, 2008). Managers can support well-being by implementing the following strategies:

1. Work-life balance: Encourage employees to maintain a healthy balance between work and personal life. Promote **flexible work** arrangements, provide resources for **managing stress**, and lead by example in **prioritizing self-care.** Leaders can promote well-being by addressing **health** needs, fostering a **fun work environment**, and supporting **work-life fit.** Lastly, considering **indi-**

vidual needs can help employees achieve a sense of fulfillment (Cascio, 2003; Chalofsky, 2010).

2. Physical health support: Offer wellness programs, fitness challenges, and access to resources that promote physical health. Encourage employees to take *breaks,* engage in *physical activity,* and adopt *healthy habits*.

3. Emotional support: Create a culture that values *emotional well-being* and supports employees in managing stress and *building resilience*. Provide access to counseling services, promote open communication, and foster a supportive peer network.

Human Resources (HR) professionals also play a crucial role in promoting positive work environments by assessing *current levels* of workplace positivity and identifying *areas for improvement* (Cascio, 2003). By providing *training to managers* on the benefits of positivity and the six essentials, HR can empower them to create a positive workplace culture (Cascio, 2003). HR professionals can also *support managers* through various programs and initiatives that *promote positivity.* This can include conducting *strengths assessments, implementing strengths-based selection processes, providing development opportunities, offering mentoring and coaching programs, promoting wellness initiatives, and implementing work-life fit strategies* (Cascio, 2003).

By focusing on what is *good, nurturing relationships*, *leveraging strengths, empowering* employees, creating *meaning,* and demonstrating genuine *concern for well-being,* organizations can cultivate **positive work cultures** where employees thrive and make meaningful contributions.

In conclusion, creating positive work environments is essential for organizational success, employee engagement, and talent retention. **Positive workplaces** go beyond financial rewards and focus on enhancing employees' **emotional well-being** and enabling them to make **meaningful contributions** (Cascio, 2003). Positive employees demonstrate improved decision-making, creativity, productivity, and interpersonal skills. By implementing the framework of workplace positivity, managers and human resource professionals can create a positive work environment that fosters success and brings about a competitive edge.

By implementing the Six Essentials of Workplace Positivity—*positive thinking, positive relationships, strengths, empowerment, meaning, and well-being* — organizations can cultivate a positive work environment where employees thrive, leading to increased engagement, productivity, and overall organizational success.

The time to start creating positive change is now.

MANAGERIAL PRACTICES FOR INCREASING WORKPLACE POSITIVITY

SIX ESSENTIALS	MANAGERIAL PRACTICES
1. Positive Thinking *Positive* *Focus* *Optimism* *Gratitude* *Forgiveness*	· Celebrate small wins · Share success stories · Focus on solutions rather than problems · Help people view negative events as temporary setbacks · Start meetings by asking people what they are thankful for · Express gratitude frequently · View mistakes as opportunities to learn
2. Positive Relationships *Respect* *Recognition* *Trust* *Generosity*	· Listen to people's ideas and opinions · Let people know you appreciate who they are · Recognize people for doing good work · Celebrate accomplishments · Act with integrity, dependability and benevolence · Encourage participation in decision making · Share information freely · Reward people for helping their colleagues · Establish a mentorship program
3. Strengths *Identify* *Use* *Develop*	· Look for rapid learning, high energy or repeated success · Administer a strengths inventory · Select individuals whose strengths fit the company's needs · Assign or modify roles to maximize strengths use · Designate a few hours each week as "strengths time" · Focus feedback on people's strengths · Provide training to further develop people's strengths
4. Empowerment *Clarity* *Support* *Autonomy*	· Clearly define goals and expectations · Provide the time and resources needed to achieve goals · Remove obstacles to success · Let people choose how to do their work
5. Meaning *Mission* *Impact* *Social responsibility*	· Continuously remind people of the company's mission · Highlight the impact people have on clients or colleagues · Communicate the company's social responsibility initiatives · Encourage participation in social responsibility programs
6. Well-being *Health* *Fun* *Work-life fit*	· Adopt wellness programs to prevent health problems · Play games, have parties, find creative ways to have fun · Offer quality of life benefits, flexible work, childcare, etc. · Work to ensure individual needs are met.

Source: Cabrera (2012).

Review

1. Experiencing positive emotions in the workplace leads to success, including better decision-making, creativity, productivity, resilience, and interpersonal skills.

2. Positivity at work is correlated with higher levels of engagement, organizational citizenship behavior, job performance, and lower burnout rates.

3. Happiness leads to success rather than the other way around.

4. Workplace positivity has six essentials: positive thinking, positive relationships, strengths, empowerment, meaning, and well-being.

5. Positive emotions broaden focus and mindset, leading to better decision-making and increased creativity.

6. Positive individuals have stronger relationships, cooperate more readily, and are more likely to help others.

7. Positivity enhances cognitive and interpersonal skills, reduces anxiety and depression, and increases motivation and resilience.

8. Positive people have better physical health, including lower blood pressure, stronger immune systems, better sleep, and less pain.

9. Individuals can intentionally increase their positivity through efforts like positive thinking, gratitude, and forgiveness.

10. Managers can create positive work environments by encouraging positive thinking, building positive relationships, leveraging strengths, empowering employees, creating meaning, and supporting well-being.

Part I: Discussion Questions

1. What are managerial skills?

2. Why are managerial skills important for personal and professional growth?

3. What type of skills are considered essential for a manager according to leadership theories?

4. Why is self-awareness considered the most critical competency for managers?

5. How can self-awareness affect relationships?

6. What is the importance of self-awareness in personal growth and effective decision-making?

7. What is the self-determination theory, and how is it related to self-awareness?

8. What are the ways to develop self-awareness?

9. What are the benefits of having a strong sense of self-awareness?

10. Why is it important for people to understand themselves and their values?

11. What is stress, and how can it affect a person's life?

12. What measures can help manage personal stress?

13. What is the difference between analytical and creative problem-solving?

14. Why is it essential to combine creative and analytical problem-solving?

15. In which areas are creative and analytical problem-solving essential?

16. How can creativity be developed in problem-solving?

17. What is the role of imagination and intuition in creative problem-solving?

18. What tools and techniques can be used in analytical problem-solving?

19. What challenges do companies face in creative and analytical problem-solving?

20. How does creative and analytical problem-solving influence the field of technology?

21. What is emotional intelligence, and how is it composed?

22. How does emotional intelligence differ from cognitive intelligence and IQ?

23. How can emotional intelligence be improved and developed?

24. What is the importance of emotional intelligence in personal and professional relationships?

25. How does E.I. affect our mental and physical health?

26. What role does E.I. play in a person's happiness and well-being?

27. Why is E.I. a critical component in effective leadership and management in the workplace?

28. How does experiencing positive emotions in the workplace contribute to success?

29. What are the six essentials of workplace positivity?

30. How do positive emotions impact decision-making and creativity?

31. What are the social benefits of positivity in the workplace?

32. How does positivity affect psychological well-being and motivation?

33. What are the health benefits associated with positivity?How can individuals increase their positivity levels?

34. What strategies can managers use to create positive work environments?

35. How does recognizing and leveraging individual strengths contribute to workplace positivity?

36. What role do managers and human resource professionals play in promoting workplace positivity?

PART II
INTERPERSONAL
MANAGEMENT SKILLS

CHAPTER 6

ASSERTIVE COMMUNICATION

"The art of communication is the language of leadership."

— James Humes

When we talk about communication, we refer to the *exchange of information between two or more people effectively and assertively,* as this is the only way to understand the message and avoid distortion. When this happens, supportive communication, or assertive communication, is being used.

Supportive communication refers to a style of communication that focuses on **empathy, understanding,** and **appreciation of others** and serves to provide **appropriate responses** and **support**. In assertive communication, one expresses **feelings, needs,** and **desires clearly** and **respectfully.**

By using supportive communication, active attention is given, understanding is shown, and emotional support is provided to the other person. This style of communication can help **improve relationships** in the workplace, personal relationships, and family relationships.

Assertive communication involves the ability to **actively listen**. Active listening means **paying attention to what the other person is saying and responding respectfully** (Gottman, 1999). Supportive communication is based on **empathy**, which is the **ability to understand and feel what another person is experiencing** (Goleman, 1998).

Active listening allows people to understand the perspectives and needs of the other person, which enables them to **communicate more effectively**. Assertive communication also includes the ability to express **respect** and **consideration**. Verbal and nonverbal expressions of respect, such as body language and words of encouragement, can help the other person feel valued and respected. These expressions can help build a relationship of trust and mutual respect (Fossum & Mason, 1986).

Supportive communication is a valuable tool for establishing healthy and lasting relationships because it is based on **mutual trust**, **respect**, and **authenticity**, i.e., the ability to be **honest** and **genuine** with others. **Authenticity** is essential for assertive communication as it allows people to express themselves **sincerely** and **genuinely**, facilitating **mutual understanding** (Brown, 2018). According to a study by Stanford University (2016), people who feel heard and understood are more likely to trust others and work effectively as a team.

Many people may have difficulty expressing themselves authentically, actively listening, or showing respect. These result from factors such as a **lack of self-confidence**, lack of communication skills, or **self-esteem issues**. Therefore, it is critical to work on these aspects to establish healthy relationship.

In the workplace, **relationships are fundamental to success**. Healthy relationships between employees and superiors can improve **team performance** and **productivity**. Supportive communication is vital in the workplace environment, as relationships can have a significant impact on employees' health and performance (Gustafsson, 2017).

Supportive communication can also help **resolve conflicts** since it focuses on **active listening**, **understanding**, and **valuing** the perspectives and contributions of others (Duggan, 2016). Individuals who use assertive communication can express their **feelings** and **needs** clearly and respectfully and seek solutions that satisfy the needs of both parties, leading to a **positive and collaborative work environment** where people feel understood, valued, and supported. According to a study by the University of California (2018), positive work relationships are related to **greater motivation**, **performance**, and **job satisfaction**. On the other hand, negative work relationships are related to higher levels of stress, anxiety, and depression.

Supportive communication is essential in personal relationships, and healthy relationships are fundamental to our **mental and physical health**. Healthy relationships can help **reduce stress** and **improve well-being** in the workplace (Riggio, 2017). Supportive communication can foster trust, understanding, and empathy (Richards, 2017). According to a study conducted by Harvard University (2015), individuals who use **assertive communication** to address conflicts are more likely to reach a **satisfactory agreement** and maintain positive relationships after the conflict. The ability to actively listen, understand and validate the feelings of others, and provide appropriate responses and support can help individuals **find solutions** that work for all parties involved.

Empathy is essential to supportive communication as it allows individuals to **connect with the emotions** and **needs** of the other person. Without empathy, it is difficult to understand the other person's perspective and provide necessary support. Active listening means paying attention to what the other person is saying and responding appropriately.

Supportive communication also includes the ability to express **affection** and understanding. **Verbal** and **nonverbal** expressions of affection, such as physical contact and words of encouragement, can help the other person feel valued and understood. These expressions can help build an emotional connection and strengthen the relationship.

Studies have shown that **communication styles** play a significant role in conflict resolution and that effective communication is critical to reaching solutions (Hart, 2019). *Assertive communication is the most effective style in resolving conflicts*, as it enables individuals to express their needs and feelings clearly while also considering the needs of others. In contrast, *passive communication* can lead to resentment and anger, while *aggressive communication* can escalate *conflicts* and damage relationships. Thus, individuals need to develop assertive communication skills to effectively resolve conflicts and build healthy relationships.

Furthermore, it would be helpful to discuss how culture can impact communication styles and relationships. *Different cultures* may have different communication norms and values, and this can affect the way people communicate and build relationships. For example, *collectivist cultures* may place more emphasis on *group harmony and relationships*, while *individualistic cultures* may prioritize *individual needs* and *autonomy* (Triandis, 1994).

Cultural differences affect how people express themselves and may require individuals to adapt their communication style to build effective relationships. Being *aware of cultural differences in communication styles* and critical for developing inter-cultural communication skills to effectively communicate and building cross-cultural relationships. Some cultures value *indirect communication*, such as metaphors or nonverbal cues, to express their thoughts and emotions, while others prefer *direct and explicit communication*. Moreover, some cultures may perceive assertive communication as *confrontational* or *disrespectful*, while others may value it as a sign of confidence and leadership. By understanding and respecting cultural differences, individuals can communicate more effectively and establish stronger relationships (Gudykunst, 2003; Hofstede, 1980).

However, supportive communication *is not always easy to achieve*. Many people may have difficulty expressing empathy, actively listening, or expressing affection. These difficulties may be the result of **emotional problems or communication problems**. Be aware of your challenges and work to improve these areas. **Practice** and **self-reflection** can help improve supportive communication and build healthy and lasting relationships.

Remember that supportive communication is not just about giving support but also about **receiving** it. Be receptive to the approval of others and open to receiving it to build healthy and lasting relationships.

In summary, supportive or assertive communication is essential for establishing lasting relationships. It is a form of communication in which one expresses their feelings, needs, and desires clearly and respectfully. **Authenticity**, **active listening**, **respect**, and **conflict management** are key elements of assertive communication. Although it can be challenging to achieve, working on these skills can significantly improve the quality of relationships.

Review

1. Communication is the effective and efficient exchange of information between two or more people.

2. Supportive communication refers to a communication style that focuses on empathy, understanding, valuing others, and providing appropriate responses and support.

3. Supportive communication is based on empathy and active listening.

4. Assertive communication is based on authenticity and the ability to be honest and genuine.

5. Difficulties in communicating assertively may result from factors such as a lack of self-confidence and communication skills, or self-esteem issues.

> *"Motivation is the art of getting people to do what you want them to do because they want to do it."*
>
> — Dwight D. Eisenhower

CHAPTER 7

MOTIVATING OTHERS

Motivation in the workplace is an important topic in personnel management, as it has a direct impact on employee productivity and performance. **Motivation** refers to the **internal and external factors that drive a person to act a certain way**. In the workplace, motivation can increase job satisfaction, reduce absenteeism and staff turnover, and improve employee productivity and performance.

There are different theories of motivation, each with its unique approach. Maslow's **hierarchy of needs** *theory* focuses on individuals' basic needs, such as safety, belonging, and self-actualization. According to Maslow, when a basic need is met, the individual seeks to fulfill the next need in the hierarchy. On the other hand, **Vroom's expectancy theory** focuses on how people perceive effort, ability, and outcome and how these factors influence motivation.

In addition to the theories mentioned above, there are other motivation theories, such as **self-determination theory**, **self-concordance theory**, and the **reward and punishment system theory**. Each of these theories offers a unique approach to motivating employees and improving their performance.

Motivating a team can be a challenging task for any leader, but it is essential to achieve success in any organization. A **motivated team is more productive and committed to the organization's goals**. Different strategies for motivating employees include setting **clear goals**, providing **autonomy**, recognizing and **rewarding success**, creating a **positive work environment**, and fostering a sense of **shared purpose**.

One of the most critical factors in motivating a team is to create a **clear vision** and **mission** for the organization. A clear **sense of purpose** helps members understand the organization's goals and how their work contributes to achieving them. According to **goal-setting theory**, specific and challenging goals lead to **higher performance** (Locke & Latham, 2002). Therefore, leaders should set **clear and measurable goals** for their teams and communicate them effectively to ensure that members understand the importance of their work. Goals and objectives provide **direction, focus**, and **purpose**, members prioritize their efforts. Additionally, goals help create a sense of ownership and responsibility among members, as they are more likely to commit to achieving the goals they helped establish.

When setting goals for your team, utilize the **S.M.A.R.T.** acronym created by George Doran, Arthur Miller, and James Cunningham. S.M.A.R.T. determines that goals must be:

Specific

Measurable

Achievable

Relevant

Time-sensitive

Another critical strategy for motivating a team is to provide **autonomy** and **empowerment**. **Autonomy** is the degree to which individuals have **control over their work** and the freedom to make decisions (Deci et al., 1999). According to self-determination theory, autonomy is a basic psychological need that must be met for individuals to be motivated (Deci & Ryan, 2000). This is because **autonomy leads to a sense of ownership and commitment and helps members feel more involved in their work**. Autonomy also leads to greater creativity and innovation, as members are more likely to propose new ideas and solutions when they have control over their work. According to Pink (2009), people often want autonomy over the task, team, technique, and time. Leaders should provide members with the **necessary resources** and **support** and then let them take the initiative to achieve the organization's goals.

Creating a **positive** and **supportive work environment** is crucial for motivating a team. A positive work environment is characterized by **trust**, **respect**, and **open communication**, where members can work in a supportive and collaborative environment (Den Hartog et al., 1999).

Leaders should foster a culture of **open communication** where members feel comfortable sharing their ideas and concerns. They should also provide opportunities for members to collaborate and work together. A positive work environment can be created through effective communication, promoting a sense of job satisfaction, building trust, and promoting a culture of open and responsive communication to feedback (Robbins & Judge, 2017).

Rewarding and **recognizing** members for their hard work is another vital strategy for motivating a team. Recognition and rewards help to create a positive work environment and can be used to recognize and celebrate team accomplishments. According to Deci et al. (1999), rewards and recognition can increase **motivation** and **performance**. Leaders should recognize and reward members for their contributions, whether through **bonuses**, **promotions**, or other forms of recognition, such as **verbal praise** and **rewards**, as they provide **tangible incentives** to achieve goals.

Leaders should create a **vision** and **mission** for the organization that **inspires** and **motivates** employees. They should communicate the organization's goals and objectives clearly and provide employees with the necessary resources and support to achieve them. Leaders should also lead by example and demonstrate the behaviors and attitudes they expect from their employees. Effective leadership can have a significant impact on employee motivation, job satisfaction, and performance (Bass, 1985). Fostering a sense of **shared purpose** is an essential strategy to motivate teams. A shared purpose helps members feel more connected to their work and see how their efforts contribute to the overall success of the organization.

A shared purpose can be fostered through **effective communication** by highlighting the importance of **teamwork** and **collaboration**. Additionally, organizations can create a sense of shared purpose by encouraging members to participate in community service projects or other activities that align with the organization's values and mission (Robbins & Judge, 2017).

One strategy for motivating employees is **providing feedback**. According to Robbins and Judge (2017), feedback is a powerful tool for improving employee performance and increasing motivation. Feedback provides employees with information about their **performance** and **areas that need improvement**, which can help them develop and grow professionally. Feedback should be given regularly and be **specific** and **constructive**, so employees can understand what they need to do to improve their performance.

Another strategy for motivating employees is to focus on **employee engagement**. Employee engagement refers to the *commitment and enthusiasm an employee has toward their work and the organization*. Engaged employees are more likely to be productive, committed, and satisfied (Saks, 2006). Leaders can foster employee engagement by providing **opportunities for growth** and **development**, recognizing and rewarding employees for their hard work, and creating a positive work environment.

Finally, *leaders should be role models for their teams by demonstrating the behaviors and attitudes they expect from team members*. According to Bass (1985), leaders have a significant impact on the motivation of their team members. Leaders should lead by example and demonstrate behaviors and attitudes such as being punctual, working hard, and being respectful of others.

Motivating a team is a complex but essential task for success in any organization. Several strategies can be used to motivate a team, including setting **clear goals**, providing **autonomy**, recognizing and **rewarding success**, creating a **positive work environment**, and fostering a sense of **shared purpose**. By using these strategies, leaders can create a motivated and committed team dedicated to achieving success. Several techniques can be used to motivate employees in the workplace:

Providing a positive and safe work environment.
Offering opportunities for professional development.
Recognizing and rewarding good performance.

Communicating clearly and openly with employees.

Providing a balance between work and personal life.

Providing fair compensation and adequate benefits.

Giving positive feedback.

Keep in mind that motivation can vary based on ***age, gender, culture,*** and other ***individual factors***. Personalize motivation strategies to fit your audience's needs and preferences.

Review

1. Motivation in the workplace is essential because it has an impact on employee productivity and performance.

2. Motivation refers to the internal and external factors that drive a person to act in a certain way.

3. Autonomy is the degree to which individuals have control over their work and freedom to make decisions.

4. Maslow's theory of needs focuses on individuals' basic needs, such as safety, belonging, and self-actualization.

5. Vroom's expectancy theory focuses on how people perceive effort, ability, and outcome and how these factors influence motivation.

6. Different motivational strategies include setting clear goals, providing autonomy, recognizing and rewarding success, creating a positive work environment, and fostering a sense of shared purpose.

7. Different strategies to motivate include setting clear goals, pro-
    viding autonomy, recognizing and rewarding success, creating
    a positive work environment, and fostering a sense of shared
    purpose.

CHAPTER 8

CONFLICT MANAGEMENT

> *"The true test of leadership is how well you function in a crisis."*
>
> — Madeleine Albright

Conflict management in the workplace is essential in personnel management because *conflicts can have a negative impact on employee productivity, performance, and morale.* Effective conflict management can help **improve communication**, **increase collaboration**, and enhance team effectiveness.

Conflict is any situation in which individuals or groups have **incompatible goals**, **interests**, or **values**. In the workplace, conflicts may occur between employees, between employees and managers, and be-tween different departments or teams. Several types of conflicts may arise in the workplace, such as **interpersonal**, **of interest**, **task con-flicts**, and **leadership style conflicts**. Each type of conflict requires a different approach to resolution.

Lewin's conflict management theory is divided into three phases: the **freezing phase**, the **thawing phase**, and the **restructur-ing phase**.

In the **freezing** phase, the *conflict is recognized and action is taken to prevent it from worsening.*

In the **thawing** phase, *solutions are sought and the terms of the agreement are negotiated.*

In the **restructuring** phase, *the solutions are implemented and progress is monitored.*

Another theory in conflict management is Thomas and Kilmann's **theory of competition and cooperation**. According to this theory, there are five styles of conflict management: (1) **competition**; (2) **avoidance**; (3) **collaboration**; (4) **compromise**; and (5) **accommoda-tion**. Each style has advantages and disadvantages, and it is vital to use the appropriate style based on the type of conflict and the needs of the parties involved.

One of the most common types of conflicts that may arise in the workplace is **interpersonal conflict**, which occurs when there are differences in personality, values, or beliefs between individuals (De

Dreu & Weingart, 2003b). Interpersonal conflicts can lead to **negative emotions**, such as **frustration**, **anger**, and **resentment**, and can have a significant impact on employee productivity and morale. To effectively manage interpersonal conflicts, it is crucial to create a **culture of respect**, *open communication*, and *empathy* in the workplace. Managers *can encourage employees to address conflicts directly with each other, provide conflict resolution training, and establish clear conflict resolution procedures.*

In addition to interpersonal conflicts, **conflicts of interest** occur when *individuals or groups have competing interests or objectives.* These conflicts can arise when employees prioritize personal interests over organizational goals or when different departments have conflicting priorities. To manage conflicts of interest effectively, managers can establish **clear goals** and **priorities** for the organization, **communicate** these priorities effectively to employees, and **encourage collaboration** and teamwork. Additionally, managers can develop **policies** and **procedures** to identify and manage conflicts of interest, such as conflict of interest disclosure forms and recusal policies (De Dreu & Weingart, 2003).

Regarding conflict management strategies in the workplace, several techniques can be used to effectively resolve conflicts. These include:

Effective communication: Listen actively and express views clearly and respectfully.

Negotiation: Seek solutions that are mutually beneficial for the parties involved.

Mediation: Use an impartial third party to help the parties reach an agreement.

Problem-solving: Using a systematic approach to identify and solve underlying problems.

Group decision-making: Involving several people in decision-making to increase buy-in and effectiveness.

Conflict management in the workplace is a crucial aspect of organizational management because *conflicts can have a **detrimental** effect on employee **productivity**, morale, and overall organizational performance.*

There are several approaches to conflict management; a popular one is the traditional **hierarchical approach**, which involves a manager or supervisor intervening to resolve the conflict. This approach can be effective when the conflicting parties cannot resolve their differences, but it can also generate resentment and power imbalances if not appropriately handled.

Another approach is the **collaborative approach**, which involves the conflicting parties working together to find a mutually beneficial solution. This approach can work in situations where the *conflicting parties have a common goal and are willing to reach an agreement* (De Dreu & Weingart, 2003).

A third approach is the **mediation approach**, which involves a neutral party to facilitate communication and negotiation between the conflicting parties. Mediation can be effective in situations where the conflicting parties are willing to work together to find a solution, but it can be challenging to implement in situations where the conflicting parties are unwilling to communicate or collaborate (Bramson & Glasser, 2017).

Regardless of the approach used, effective conflict management involves several key steps. These include:

Identify the source of the conflict: To effectively manage a conflict, seek to understand the underlying causes of the conflict. This may involve conducting interviews with the conflicting parties, observing interactions, or gathering other relevant information (Kwok & Wang, 2018).

Communicate effectively: Effective communication is crucial for resolving conflicts. This involves active listening, expressing oneself clearly, and providing constructive feedback (Kwok & Wang, 2018).

Find common ground: One of the most vital steps in resolving conflicts is finding common ground between the conflicting parties by identifying shared goals, interests, or values (De Dreu & Weingart, 2003).

Brainstorm solutions: Once common ground has been established, brainstorm to find possible solutions to the conflict. This may include having the conflicting parties work together to develop an action plan or may involve a third party to facilitate the process (Bramson & Glasser, 2017).

Implement the solution: Once a solution has been identified, implement it in a timely and effective manner. This may involve setting clear goals and deadlines, assigning responsibilities, and monitoring progress.

Evaluate the outcome: Once a solution has been implemented, evaluate its effectiveness. This may involve conducting follow-up interviews or surveys with the conflicting parties, or tracking performance metrics (Kwok & Wang, 2018).

In conclusion, conflict management in the workplace is an essential topic that can have a significant impact on organizational performance. Effective conflict management involves *identifying the source of the conflict, communicating effectively, finding common ground, generating solutions, implementing the resolution, and evaluating the outcome.* It is important to note that conflicts can take different forms and have various causes, such as interpersonal, structural, and interest conflicts. Understanding the type of conflict can help managers choose the appropriate approach to managing it.

Review

1. Effective conflict management can help improve communication, increase collaboration, and enhance teamwork effectiveness.

2. Workplace conflicts can be caused by various factors, such as interpersonal conflicts, conflicts of interest, task conflicts, and leadership style conflicts.

3. Lewin's conflict management theory is divided into three phases: freezing, unfreezing, and restructuring.

4. Thomas and Kilmann's theory of competition and cooperation mentions five conflict management styles: competition, avoidance, collaboration, compromise, and accommodation.

5. Workplace conflict management strategies include effective communication, negotiation, mediation, problem-solving, and group decision-making.

6. A popular approach to workplace conflict management is the traditional hierarchical approach, where a manager or supervisor intervenes to resolve the conflict.

7. Another approach to conflict management is the collaborative approach, where conflicting parties work together to find a mutually beneficial solution.

8. A third approach is the mediation approach, which involves the use of a neutral third party to facilitate communication and negotiation between conflicting parties.

9. Conflict management in the workplace can have a detrimental effect on employee productivity, morale, and overall organizational performance.

Part II: Discussion Questions

1. What is supportive communication, and how does it differ from other forms of communication?

2. How can supportive communication help establish healthy and lasting relationships?

3. What are the critical characteristics of assertive communication?

4. What is the importance of active listening in supportive communication?

5. What role does empathy play in supportive communication?

6. Why is the expression of respect and consideration important in assertive communication?

7. What is the importance of authenticity in assertive communication?

8. What difficulties can arise in supportive communication, and how can they be addressed?

9. How can supportive communication influence the performance and productivity of a team in the workplace?

10. How can supportive communication improve relationships in the home and personal relationships?

11. What is workplace motivation, and what is its impact on employee productivity and performance?

12. What are the most well-known theories of motivation, and what is their unique approach?

13. Why is it important to motivate a team in an organization?

14. How can leaders establish clear and measurable goals for their team to improve motivation?

15. What is the role of autonomy and empowerment in motivating team members?

16. What are some effective strategies for motivating employees in the workplace?

17. What impact does a sense of purpose have on team motivation?

18. How does goal-setting influence the performance and commitment of team members?

19. What role does self-determination theory play in employee motivation?

20. What is the importance of creating a positive work environment to motivate employees?

21. What are the adverse effects that can arise from conflicts in the workplace?

22. What is Lewin's conflict management theory, and how is it divided into three phases?

23. What is Thomas and Kilmann's theory of competition and cooperation, and what are the five conflict management styles mentioned in this theory?

24. What conflict management strategies are effective in the workplace?

25. What is the traditional hierarchical approach, and what are its advantages and disadvantages in managing conflicts in the workplace?

26. What is the collaborative approach, and what are its advantages and disadvantages in managing conflicts in the workplace?

27. How can effective communication helpful with managing conflicts in the workplace?

28. How can negotiation help to resolve conflicts in the workplace?

29. What are the challenges associated with mediation in managing conflicts in the workplace?

30. How can group decision-making be an effective strategy for managing conflicts in the workplace?

PART III
TEAM
MANAGEMENT SKILLS

> *"If you want to do a few small things right, do them yourself. If you want to do great things and make a big impact, learn to delegate."*
>
> — John Maxwell

CHAPTER 9

EMPOWERMENT & DELEGATION

Empowerment and delegation are two vital aspects of effective team management (Goleman, Boyatzis, & McKee, 2002). **Empowerment** refers to *the process of giving team members the authority, resources, and support necessary to make decisions and take action* (Kouzes & Posner, 2007). On the other hand, **delegation** is *the act of entrusting specific tasks or responsibilities*. Together, these two concepts can help teams achieve their goals, improve performance, and increase job satisfaction (Buckingham & Coffman, 1999).

79

Empowerment is a critical factor in creating a sense of belonging and commitment among team members. When members feel that they have a say in decisions that affect them, they are more likely to **take ownership** of their work and feel a **sense of responsibility** for the team's success (Costa & McCrae, 1992; Northouse, 2016). This sense of belonging and commitment can lead to **increased productivity**, **better performance**, and a higher level of **job satisfaction**. Empowerment also allows members to develop **new skills** and take on **new responsibilities,** which can lead to personal and professional growth (Furnham, 2006; Deci & Ryan, 2000).

Delegation is an essential aspect of effective team management. When done correctly, delegation can help **reduce workload**, **increase productivity**, and **improve performance**. By **delegating** tasks and responsibilities to members, managers can leverage the **unique strengths** and **skills** of each team member and ensure that tasks are completed in a **timely** and **efficient** manner. Additionally, delegation can help develop the **leadership skills** of members, who will have the opportunity to assume more responsibility and authority in decision-making (Northouse, 2016; Robbins & Judge, 2017).

Influential leaders empower and delegate to their teams and create a **sense of belonging** and **commitment** among members. **Effective delegation** requires clear **communication, goals** and **expectations**, and **trust** between the manager and members. Leaders must **communicate their expectations clearly** and ensure that members understand the objectives and goals of the task or project. They must also provide the **necessary resources** and support for members to successfully complete the task. Additionally, managers must **trust their members** to complete the job to the best of their ability and be willing to provide **guidance** and **support** as needed, which helps create a positive and productive work environment.

To effectively empower and delegate to teams, *managers must first understand the skills and strengths of each member.* This can be achieved through regular communication, performance evaluations, and team-building activities. *By understanding the **skills** and **strengths** of each member, managers can **delegate tasks** and **responsibilities** that best fit each individual and provide the necessary resources and support for them to successfully complete the task* (Robbins & Judge, 2017; Northouse, 2016).

One of the main barriers to effective delegation is the **fear of losing control.** Managers who struggle with delegation may believe that they are the only ones who can complete tasks correctly, which may lead to **micromanagement** and hinder team performance. To overcome this barrier, managers need to **trust their team members** and provide them with the necessary resources and support to complete tasks effectively.

Another challenge that managers may face is identifying **which tasks to delegate**. Managers must be able to identify tasks that are best suited for delegation and those that require their direct involvement. *This requires a clear understanding of each team member's strengths, skills, and expertise.* Additionally, managers must ensure that team members have the necessary resources and support to complete tasks effectively.

Finally, **language and cultural barriers** can also present challenges to effective delegation in diverse teams. Managers must be aware of these barriers and provide clear communication and instructions to team members to ensure that tasks are completed effectively.

Managers can implement various strategies to address these challenges, such as providing **clear expectations**, setting **realistic goals**, establishing **checkpoints**, and providing **constructive feedback** (Robbins & Judge, 2017). Additionally, managers can provide training and development opportunities to team members to enhance their skills and knowledge, which can also lead to increased job satisfaction (Deci & Ryan, 2000).

Effective leaders can delegate in eight different ways:

1. *They choose the right person, and it's not always about who can do it.* Who needs to develop these skills? Who has the capacity? Who has shown interest? Who is ready for a challenge? Who would see this as a reward? Successful delegators also explain why they chose that person to carry out the task.

2. *They are clear about what that person is responsible for and how much autonomy they have.* In the book "Drive: The Surprising Science About What Motivates Us," Daniel Pink writes that people often want autonomy over the task, the team, the technique, and the time. Successful delegators let their members know exactly where they have independence

and where they do not (yet).

3. ***They describe the desired results in detail.*** This includes setting clear expectations about the outcome ("what is"), how the task relates to the big picture ("why we are doing it"), and the criteria for measuring success ("how it should look when done right").

4. ***They ensure that members have the necessary resources to do the job,*** whether it's training, money, supplies, time, a private space, adjusted priorities, or help from others.

5. ***They establish checkpoints,*** milestones, and moments for feedback to avoid micromanagement or poor leadership.

6. ***They encourage new and creative ways for members to achieve their goals.*** It is crucial for delegators to set aside their attachment to how things have been done in the past so that they can invite, recognize, and reward novel approaches that work.

7. ***They create a motivating environment.*** Successful delegators know when to applaud, advise, intervene, step back, adjust expectations, be available, and celebrate successes.

8. ***They tolerate risks and mistakes and use them as learning opportunities*** instead of seeing them as proof that they shouldn't have delegated in the first place. Good delegation helps leaders maximize their resources, ensuring they focus

on their highest priorities, develop their members, and create a culture where delegation is not only expected but embedded.

In conclusion, **empowerment** and **delegation** are vital for effective team management. Empowerment creates a **sense of belonging** and **commitment** among members and allows them to develop new skills and take on new responsibilities. Delegation helps **reduce workload**, **increase productivity**, and **improve performance**. Managers must understand each member's skills and strengths to delegate tasks effectively and enable their teams to achieve their goals.

Together, these two concepts can help teams achieve their goals, improve performance, and increase job satisfaction.

Review

1. Effective leaders tolerate risks and mistakes and use them as learning opportunities.

2. Empowerment refers to giving members the authority, resources, and support to make decisions.

3. Delegation is the act of entrusting tasks or responsibilities to members.

4. Empowerment is a critical factor in creating a sense of belonging and commitment among members.

5. Delegation can help reduce workload, increase productivity, and

improve performance.

6. Effective leaders are those who can enable and delegate to their teams and create a sense of belonging and commitment.

7. To delegate effectively to teams, managers must first understand each member's skills and strengths.

8. Managers can implement various strategies to address these challenges, such as providing clear expectations, setting realistic goals, establishing checkpoints, and providing constructive feedback.

CHAPTER 10

TEAM BUILDING

A team — a small number of people with complementary skills — is the *primary unit of productivity in high-performance organizations*. According to Robbins and Judge (2017), team building is the process of creating and maintaining a **cohesive**, **high-performing** team by developing **trust**, **communication**, and **shared goals** among members. This process involves a variety of activities, such as team-building exercises, training, and communication, which are designed to enhance performance and productivity (Kozlowski & Ilgen, 2006).

Team building is a necessary component of effective team management because it helps to create a **sense of unity** and **purpose** among members, leading to **better performance** and greater **job satisfaction** (Northouse, 2016). Team building can be used to achieve different goals, such as improving **communication**, increasing **productivity**, and enhancing **cohesion**, that is, the degree of unity and cooperation within a team (Robbins & Judge, 2017).

In an article published in the *Harvard Business Review* titled "The Discipline of Teams," Jon R. Katzenbach and Douglas K. Smith discuss the characteristics of a team and the elements that make it function effectively:

1. *Meaningful common purpose*
2. *Specific performance goals*
3. *A mix of complementary skills*
4. *Strong commitment to how work is done*
5. *Mutual accountability*

Top management must recognize a team's unique potential to **deliver results**, **deploy teams strategically**, and foster the **basic discipline** of teams to enable team as well as individual and organizational performance.

Teams must have shared ownership of their purpose and goals, inspiring and challenging team members so the team reaches performance levels greater than their individual bests. Here are some ideas to build your team:

1. ***Establish urgency,*** performance standards, and direction for the team.

2. ***Select team members based on their skills*** and potential for improvement.

3. ***Carefully plan the first meetings*** as they set the tone for the team.

4. ***Set rules of behavior,*** including attendance, discussion, confidentiality, and constructive confrontation.

5. ***Set immediate performance-oriented tasks*** and goals to achieve early success.

6. ***Challenge the team regularly*** with new facts and information to improve understanding and approach.

7. ***Spend time together,*** both scheduled and unscheduled, to bond and develop as a team.

8. ***Use positive feedback,*** recognition, and reward to shape new behaviors and encourage contributions.

Set performance goals that help your team focus and communicate clearly, laying a firm foundation for team success. Creating a **team charter** outlining the team's *purpose, goals, expectations, meeting times, modes of communication, individual strengths, and roles* is vital for the team's success.

One of the challenges of team building is addressing **conflicts** that may arise among team members. Conflicts can arise *due to dif-*

ferences in personalities, communication styles, or goals. To address these conflicts, team leaders can use conflict resolution techniques such as **mediation**, **negotiation**, and **compromise**. Additionally, team leaders can establish ground rules for communication and collaboration that promote respectful and effective communication among team members (Groysberg, Lee, & Nohria, 2008).

Another **challenge** in team building is the **formation of cliques**, where team members form exclusive groups and exclude others from participating fully in team activities. To address this issue, team leaders can encourage **cross-functional collaboration**, where team members from different departments or roles work together on projects. Team leaders can also use team-building exercises that enable members to work with various team members, which can help break down barriers and increase collaboration among team members (Hoegl & Gemuenden, 2001).

Moreover, team building is also affected by the **diversity** of team members, which can lead to communication and coordination challenges. To address these challenges, team leaders can provide training and education on cultural **sensitivity**, which can help team members better **understand** and **appreciate** each other's differences. Additionally, team leaders can use team-building exercises that promote **diversity and inclusivity**, such as celebrating **cultural events** and highlighting the contributions of diverse team members. Team building and training are crucial components of effective team management (Mor Barak, Cherin, & Berkman, 1998).

By addressing challenges such as conflicts, cliques, and diversity, team leaders can build **cohesive and high-performing teams** that achieve their goals and contribute to the organization's success. Effective communication is fundamental to building a cohesive and efficient team, according to Kouzes and Posner (2007). It allows members to share information, ideas, and feedback and coordinate their efforts. *Good communication also fosters a sense of belonging and commitment among members.* Communication can be improved through team-building activities such as meetings, training sessions, and social events (Cameron & Quinn, 2006).

When members communicate effectively with each other, share ideas, collaborate on projects, and solve problems together, **better performance** and greater **job satisfaction** are the natural results. It can result in better decision-making, increased productivity, and better performance. When members can work together effectively, **they can achieve more than they could individually**. Team-building activities can help to improve performance by providing opportunities for members to learn new skills and work together on projects (Deci & Ryan, 2000).

"Innovation is a process of discovery," conclude Furr and Dyer (2014). The process of creating an innovative teamwork approach has four steps:

1. Generate insights into problems worth solving by asking questions, observing, and networking.

2. Identify a significant unsolved problem or unfulfilled need worth pursuing.

3. Develop the solution, starting with a theoretical **prototype**, then a virtual prototype, followed by a minimum viable prototype, and finally, a pilot test of the final solution.

4. Devise the business model through **experimentation**, including pricing and customer acquisition, using the same approach in developing the solution.

It's essential to work through each step judiciously before scaling, even for organizations with network effects. By combining **risk-reduction ideas** from innovation thinkers and practitioners, organizations can significantly increase their chances of success in launching new ideas.

Shared goals are critical for team building. When members share a common purpose and understand how their efforts contribute to the team's overall goals, they are more likely to work together effectively. Setting **clear and measurable goals** and regularly reviewing progress toward these goals can help increase **motivation** and **commitment** among members (Kozlowski & Ilgen, 2006).

Team-building **exercises** are *activities designed to improve team performance by building trust, improving communication, and promoting collaborative work*. These exercises can take many forms, such as **trust-building**, **problem-solving**, and **team challenge** exercises. By participating in team-building exercises, members can develop **new skills** and improve their ability to **work together**, leading to better performance and greater job satisfaction (Furnham, 2006; Bass, 1990).

In addition to communication and formation exercises, **training** is also an essential aspect of team building. One such strategy is to provide members with opportunities for **skills development** and **growth.** This may include training and development programs and opportunities for members to take on new roles and responsibilities. Training is an effective way to build an efficient team because it allows members to **learn new skills** and **improve their abilities**. By providing members with the necessary training, managers can ensure that members have the skills and knowledge they need to perform their jobs effectively, leading to better performance.

Team training should also include opportunities for members to **bond** and **build relationships** outside of work. This can consist of team-building activities, such as **retreats** and **social events**. These activities can help members get to know each other on a personal level, which can lead to better communication and trust among members (Kozlowski & Ilgen, 2006).

Effective team training also involves creating an **inclusive** and **diverse environment** that values the contributions of all members. This includes actively **recruiting** and **promoting** a diverse workforce and creating an environment where all members feel comfortable expressing their ideas and opinions. A diverse team can bring a **variety** of **perspectives** and **skills**, which can lead to better decision-making and problem-solving (Robbins & Judge, 2017).

One of the key benefits of team training is the **development of trust** among members. Trust is the belief in the **reliability, integrity, and ability** of members. When members trust each other, they are more likely to share information, collaborate, and support each other. Trust also leads to better communication, which is essential for effective team functioning (Cameron and Quinn, 2006; Kozlowski & Ilgen, 2006).

Another strategy is to provide members with **regular feedback** on their performance. This includes **positive feedback** to recognize a job well done, as well as **constructive feedback** to help members improve and grow in their roles. Additionally, managers should create an environment that fosters open and honest communication and encourages members to share their ideas and concerns.

In conclusion, team building is an essential aspect of successful organizations. It involves *creating and maintaining a cohesive, high-performing team by developing trust, communication, and shared goals among members*. Critical elements for successful team building include *trust, effective communication, shared goals, skill development, regular feedback, building bonds and relationships, and fostering an inclusive and diverse environment.*

By implementing these strategies, organizations can create effective teams to achieve their goals and succeed in today's competitive organizational environment.

Review

1. Team building is the process of creating and maintaining a cohesive and high-performing team by developing trust, communication, and shared goals among members.

2. Team building is a necessary component of effective team management because it helps create a sense of unity and purpose.

3. Team building can be used to achieve a variety of objectives, such as improving communication, increasing productivity, and enhancing team cohesion.

4. Cohesion refers to the degree of unity and cooperation within a team.

5. One of the challenges of team building is addressing conflicts that may arise among team members. Conflicts can occur due to differences in personalities, communication styles, or goals.

6. Team leaders can encourage cross-functional collaboration, where team members from different departments or roles work together on projects.

7. According to Kouzes and Posner (2007), effective communication is fundamental to building a cohesive and efficient team. Good communication also fosters a sense of belonging and commitment among members.

8. When members can work together effectively, they can achieve more than they could individually.

9. When members share a common purpose and understand how their individual efforts contribute to the team's overall goals, they are more likely to work together effectively.

CHAPTER 11

CHAPTER 11

LEADING POSITIVE CHANGE

"Be the change you wish to see in the world."

— Gandhi

The ability to lead positive change is a critical skill for any leader. Positive change is defined as a ***change that results in an improvement of the current situation or condition***. Positive change can be implemented in various scenarios, such as organizations, communities, and society in general. To lead positive change, a leader must possess specific characteristics and skills and be able to apply various strategies and methods (Schermerhorn, Hunt, & Osborn, 2017).

As discussed above, one of the essential characteristics of a leader who can lead positive change is **emotional intelligence** (E.I.) To recap, emotional intelligence is the *ability to perceive, understand, and manage emotions in oneself and others*. A leader with high E.I. can empathize with others, understand their perspectives, and respond to their needs and concerns. This allows the leader to create a positive and supportive environment in which change can take place. Additionally, a leader with high E.I. can better **manage stress** and maintain a **positive attitude**, crucial for leading change in a challenging and uncertain environment (Salovey & Mayer, 1990; Goleman, 1998).

Another characteristic of a leader who can effect positive change is **visionary leadership**, which Senge (1990) defines as the *ability to inspire and guide others to achieve a shared vision*. A visionary leader can create a **clear** and **compelling vision of the future** that inspires and motivates others to take action. They can communicate their vision in a way that **connects with people** and makes them feel part of the change, creating a sense of **shared purpose** and **belonging,** leading to positive change.

An effective leader also needs to create a sense of urgency. This means that the leader must be able to communicate the need for change in a way that creates a **sense of urgency** and inspires people to take action. The leader can create this sense of urgency by communicating the **need for change** (Kotter, 1996). Another effective strategy is to instill a **sense of hope** by sharing a clear and compelling vision of the future that inspires people to believe that **change is possible** (Cameron & Green, 2015). By doing this, the leader can generate a sense of **confidence** and **optimism** in their team, which is essential for leading positive change.

A sense of belonging can be fostered by **involving people** in the change process and giving them a **sense of responsibility** for the outcome (Lencioni, 2002). This creates a sense of **commitment** and **dedication** is essential for leading positive changes.

Stakeholders are more likely to support the change if they are involved in the **planning** and **execution** of the change (Burke, 2008). This gives them a sense of participation and control over the change process, which increases their commitment and motivation. Additionally, it is important to be **transparent** and keep people informed about the progress of the change (Kotter, 1996), which helps reduce resistance to change and improves employees' perception.

A leader will not be able to effect positive change without a **solid work ethic**. Ethical leadership involves demonstrating ethical principles and values such as **honesty**, **integrity**, **fairness**, and **responsibility** (Brown & Treviño, 2006). ***Ethical leaders inspire trust and confidence in their followers and create a culture of accountability and ethical behavior.*** Moral leadership is crucial when change may involve **ethical dilemmas** or trade-offs between short-term gains and long-term sustainability. An ethical leader must be able to **align the change effort** with the organization's **values** and **principles** and ensure that the change is carried out **responsibly** and **sustainably** (Voegtlin & Greenwood, 2016).

Furthermore, the leader must build a ***strong coalition of support***. This requires the leader to identify ***key stakeholders*** and involve them in the change effort. The leader must be able to communicate the vision and values of the change effort to stakeholders and build a ***sense of ownership*** and ***commitment*** to the change. Leaders must also have a ***follow-up strategy*** to ensure that the change is implemented effectively. This includes ***monitoring*** and ***evaluating*** progress, making necessary adjustments, and recognizing employees' achievements and contributions. It is also essential for leaders to provide support and resources to help employees adapt to change and achieve goals (Burke, 2008).

However, leading positive change can also present challenges. For example, the leader must be able to ***manage resistance to change***. Leaders must have ***persuasion*** and ***negotiation skills*** to overcome ***resistance*** and align employees with the organization's vision and goals. Change is often accompanied by resistance, and it is the leader's responsibility to address and effectively manage resistance. This requires the leader to understand the sources of resistance and develop strategies to overcome it. This can be achieved through ***effective communication***, ***collaboration***, and ***involving stakeholders*** in the decision-making process.

Leaders must also be ***flexible*** and ***willing to adapt*** to changes and challenges, facing and overcoming resistance to change, both internal and external to the organization (Burke, 2008). They must also balance the need for change with maintaining ***continuity*** and ***stability*** in the organization (Kotter, 1996).

In summary, E.I. is a ***sine qua non*** of positive change, enabling leaders to understand and manage their own emotions as well as the emotions of others. With the right skills and strategies — such as a ***strong work ethic, honesty, integrity, fairness,*** and ***responsibility*** — leaders can successfully navigate the challenges of leading positive changes and steer the organization toward success.

Review

1. Positive change is defined as a change that results in an improvement of the current situation or condition.

2. To lead positive change, a leader must also possess certain skills, such as emotional intelligence, which is the ability to perceive, understand, and manage emotions in oneself and others.

3. A leader with high emotional intelligence can empathize with others, understand their perspectives, and respond to their concerns. This allows the leader to create a positive and supportive environment in which change can take place.

4. Visionary leadership is the ability to inspire and guide others to achieve a shared vision.

5. The leader must communicate the need for change in a way that creates a sense of urgency and inspires people to take action.

6. An ethical leader creates a sense of hope by communicating a clear and compelling vision of the future that inspires people to believe that change is possible.

7. It is vital to be transparent and keep people informed about the progress of the change to reduce resistance to the change and improve employees' perception of the change.

8. Remember to maintain open and effective communication with the people affected by the change.

Part III: Discussion Questions

1. What is empowerment, and how can it affect team members?

2. How can delegation improve team performance and productivity?

3. How are empowerment and delegation related to effective leadership?

4. What is necessary to achieve effective delegation, and how can it influence the work environment?

5. What is the importance of understanding team members' skills and strengths to empower them and delegate effectively?

6. Why is training in effective team management so valuable?

7. How can team training improve communication?

8. What benefits can a well-trained team achieve?

9. How can shared goals help a team work together effectively?

10. What is the role of team-building exercises?

11. Why is cohesion crucial in a team, and how can it be improved through team training?

12. How can team training improve motivation and commitment among team members?

13. What role do social events play in the team-building process?

14. How can team meetings improve communication within a team?

15. Why is training necessary in the team-building process?

16. What is positive change, and how can it be led?

17. What is the importance of emotional intelligence in leading positive change?

18. How can a leader be visionary and motivate their team to work toward a shared vision?

19. What is the importance of creating a sense of urgency and hope in leading positive change?

20. What role does employee participation play in the planning and execution of change?

21. How can a leader keep their employees informed and reduce resistance to change?

22. What is the importance of building a strong coalition of support in leading positive change?

PART IV
ORGANIZATIONAL MANAGEMENT SKILLS

CHAPTER 12

STRATEGIC THINKING

> "Efforts and courage are not enough without purpose and direction."
>
> — John F. Kennedy

Business management involves *making decisions that affect the long-term success of an organization*. According to Grant (2019), strategic thinking is the process of *"formulating objectives, making decisions, and taking actions that determine the long-term performance of an organization"* (p. 3). Strategic thinking is a complex cognitive process that requires managers to think beyond the present and **envision the future** possibilities of an organization (Ireland & Hitt, 2005).

Strategic thinking involves **evaluating** and **analyzing** data, **assessing risks** and opportunities, developing a **long-term plan**, and **adapting to changing circumstances**. It is a way of thinking that considers the big picture, takes into account the organization's internal and external environment, and guides decision-making to achieve the organization's long-term goals. Strategic thinking involves anticipating **future challenges** and **opportunities** and creating a **plan of action** to achieve long-term goals (Schwenk, 1984). In other words, strategic thinking is about **thinking ahead** and **taking a proactive approach** to decision-making and planning.

Strategic thinking helps organizations to develop and achieve their long-term goals. It involves a **proactive approach** to decision-making and planning, taking into account both internal and external factors that can impact an organization's success. Strategic thinking also enables organizations to **align their resources** and **capabilities** with their long-term goals, which can help to increase their **competitiveness** and **sustainability**. Moreover, strategic thinking can help organizations to navigate uncertain and complex environments and adapt to changing circumstances (Grant, 2019).

In addition, strategic thinking helps managers align the organization's **resources** and **capabilities** with its **long-term goals**, creating a sustainable competitive advantage (Porter, 1996). Moreover, strategic thinking fosters **innovation** and **creativity**, which can lead to the development of new products, services, and business models (Christensen, 1997).

To apply strategic thinking, managers must first define the organization's **long-term** goals and **vision** and then develop a plan that outlines the steps needed to achieve these goals. This plan should take into account the organization's **strengths, weaknesses, opportunities,** and **threats (S.W.O.T.)** and consider the external environment, including **market trends**, **competitors**, and **regulatory issues**. In addition, the plan should be **flexible** enough to adapt to changing circumstances and be **communicated effectively** throughout the organization to ensure **buy-in** and support from all stakeholders.

Strategic thinking is not an innate ability; rather, it is a skill that **can be developed** and honed over time. To develop strategic thinking skills, managers must cultivate a **growth mindset,** be open to learning, and continuously seek new information and perspectives (Dweck, 2006). Additionally, managers must have a deep understanding of their organization's **vision, mission, values,** and **goals**, as well as its internal and external environment. This understanding allows managers to make **informed decisions** and take **calculated risks** that align with the organization's strategic direction.

There are several strategies that individuals and organizations can use to develop strategic thinking. Firstly, individuals can improve their strategic thinking skills *by reading widely, attending training programs, and seeking feedback from others*. They can also develop their ability to **think critically** and **creatively** by **challenging assumptions**, **exploring alternatives**, and considering **multiple perspectives**.

Secondly, organizations can foster strategic thinking by *creating a culture that values innovation, risk-taking, and continuous learning*. They can also **encourage collaboration** and **communication** across different departments and levels of the organization to ensure that everyone is aligned with the organization's goals and vision. By **thinking strategically**, managers can *identify potential risks* and opportunities, develop decision-making processes *to mitigate risks* and *capitalize on opportunities*, and ensure that the organization is moving in the right direction.

The use of **data analytics** has become increasingly crucial in strategic thinking as businesses strive to gain a **competitive advantage** in today's rapidly evolving environment. Data analytics involves *using statistical techniques to extract meaningful insights from data and make informed decisions*. Data analytics can help businesses to gain a better understanding of their customers, competitors, and the market (Hess & Bacouel-Jentjens, 2018).

By analyzing customer data, businesses can **identify trends**, **preferences**, and **behaviors**, which can be used to create personalized marketing campaigns and improve customer experience. Data analytics also analyzes **competitors' strategies**, **market trends**, and **emerging technologies**, allowing businesses to stay ahead of the curve and seize opportunities. In addition, data analytics can help businesses to make informed decisions and mitigate risks (Schwenk, 1984).

Moreover, data analytics can help businesses to *identify operational inefficiencies and areas for improvement* (Hess & Bacouel-Jentjens, 2018). By analyzing internal data, businesses can identify **bottlenecks, waste,** and **other inefficiencies** in their processes and develop strategies to improve efficiency and reduce costs. For example, by analyzing data on production processes, a manufacturing company can identify areas where productivity can be improved and waste reduced, ultimately leading to **increased profitability**.

By analyzing **consumer behavior, market trends**, and other factors, businesses can **develop forecasts** and scenarios that allow them to **anticipate** and **prepare** for potential **challenges**. Data analytics can evaluate the potential impact of **strategic decisions**, allowing businesses to make informed decisions and minimize risks. Overall, data analytics can play a **critical role** in strategic thinking by providing businesses with the **insights** and **information** they need to make *informed decisions* and achieve their objectives.

However, to leverage the full potential of data analytics, *businesses must have the* **right tools, resources,** *and* **expertise.** One of the challenges of data analytics is the sheer **volume** and **complexity** of data available. This requires **investments in technology** and **infrastructure**, as well as the expertise to use these tools effectively. Businesses must also have a clear understanding of their data and how it can be used to support their strategic objectives.

Moreover, organizations must have the **right talent** to leverage data analytics effectively. Data **analysts** and **scientists** play a critical role in helping businesses to extract insights from data and make informed decisions. These professionals must have the **right skills** and **knowledge** to analyze data effectively and communicate insights to decision-makers. Furthermore, *businesses must foster a culture of* **data-driven decision-making,** *where insights from data are integrated into strategic planning and decision-making processes* (Hess & Bacouel-Jentjens, 2018).

Culture shapes an individual's beliefs, attitudes, and behaviors, including their approach to strategic thinking. According to the **cultural dimensions theory** developed by Hofstede (1984), six dimensions of culture can influence strategic thinking:

1. *Power distance*
2. *Individualism versus collectivism*
3. *Uncertainty avoidance*
4. *Masculinity vs. femininity*
5. *Long-term versus short-term orientation*
6. *Indulgence versus restraint*

Power distance refers to the extent to which individuals in a culture *accept and expect an unequal distribution of power*, which can affect how they approach decision-making and planning. In a culture with high power distance, individuals may defer to authority figures and rely on established practices, while in a culture with low power distance, individuals may value collaboration and innovation (Hofstede, 1984). High power distance cultures found in Asia and Latin America show a greater acceptance of hierarchical structures and respect for authority. In contrast, low power distance cultures, such as those in Nordic countries, emphasize more egalitarianism and less power differentials.

Individualism versus collectivism refers to *how much people identify as part of a group or as individuals.* Individualistic cultures, such as those found in the United States and Western Europe, emphasize personal achievement and individual rights, while those found in East Asia value harmony and cooperation.

Uncertainty avoidance reflects the *extent to which a society feels threatened by ambiguity and uncertainty.* Cultures with high uncertainty avoidance, such as those found in Japan and Greece, tend to have strict codes of behavior and resistance to change, while cultures with low uncertainty avoidance (e.g., Denmark and Sweden) are more comfortable with change and ambiguity.

Masculinity versus femininity refers to the *extent to which a culture **values traditional masculine traits**, such as assertiveness and competitiveness, versus traditional feminine traits, such as nurturing and cooperation.* Cultures with high masculinity (e.g., Japan and Germany) value assertiveness and competition, while the Nordic countries value cooperation and social welfare.

Long-term versus short-term orientation reflects the *extent to which a culture values future-oriented behaviors, such as saving*

and planning, versus present-oriented behaviors, such as immediate gratification. Cultures with a long-term orientation, such as
those found in China and Japan, value **saving** and **investing**, while
those with a short-term orientation (e.g., the United States and Can-
ada) value immediate results and quick gratification.

Indulgence versus restraint reflects how much a culture allows
for the gratification of natural human desires and impulses. High
indulgence cultures are those found in Latin America and the Ca-
ribbean, which are more relaxed and accepting of leisure time and
enjoyment, while those found in East Asia place a greater emphasis
on self-control and restraint (Hofstede, 2011).

Social factors such as **socioeconomic status**, **education level**,
and **peer influence** can also impact strategic thinking. Individuals
with a higher socioeconomic status may have greater access to resources and opportunities, allowing them to approach decision-making and planning differently than those with a lower socioeconomic
status. Similarly, individuals with higher education levels may have
different approaches to decision-making and planning than those
with lower education levels. **Peer influence** can also shape strategic
thinking, as individuals may be influenced by the beliefs, attitudes,
and behaviors of those in their social circles.

The impact of cultural and social factors on strategic thinking
can be addressed through various strategies. One strategy is to **raise
awareness of cultural** and **social influences** on strategic thinking by
providing training and education on cultural dimensions, diversity,

and inclusion. This can help individuals to recognize and understand different approaches to decision-making and planning, leading to more effective collaboration and innovation. For example, a study by Ryan, Arnold, and Tindall (2015) found that **cross-cultural training** improved strategic thinking and decision-making in multinational teams.

Another strategy is to **promote diversity and inclusion** in decision-making and planning processes by ensuring that individuals from **diverse backgrounds** and **perspectives** are included. This can help to counteract the influence of cultural and social factors by allowing for a broader range of ideas and approaches to be considered. For example, a study by Rink, Harvey, and Thompson (2017) found that *team diversity in decision-making teams improved strategic thinking and decision-making quality.*

A third strategy is to *foster a culture of open communication and collaboration by encouraging individuals to share their perspectives, challenge assumptions, and consider alternatives.* This can help to overcome the influence of cultural and social factors by promoting a more **open and innovative approach** to **decision-making** and planning (Mathe and Scott-Ladd, 2016). This requires a proactive approach to decision-making and planning, taking into account both **internal** and **external factors** that can impact an organization's success.

Scenario planning is a way of thinking that *considers a range of possible outcomes and explores the potential consequences of* *different actions and decisions.* It can be a powerful tool for organizations to **identify** different plausible futures, and **anticipate** and **prepare** for them (Schoemaker, 1995). Scenario planning helps organizations to develop **contingency plans** and identify **potential risks** and **opportunities**, leading to informed decisions and a proactive approach to planning and decision-making.

Scenario planning has several advantages over traditional strategic planning methods by encouraging organizations to think more broadly and deeply about the future and to consider a wider range of possible outcomes. This can help organizations to identify **blind spots** and avoid being caught off guard by unexpected events. Scenario planning makes organizations more **flexible** and **resilient** when facing challenges (Rohrbeck et al., 2013; Dreyer & Gronhaug, 2014).

Scenario planning involves several steps, including *identifying the scope of the scenario planning exercise, developing plausible scenarios, analyzing the potential impacts of each scenario, and developing plans and actions to address the potential risks and opportunities.* The scope of the scenario planning exercise should be defined based on the organization's objectives and the potential risks and opportunities it may face in the future. The **plausible scenarios** should be *based on a range of factors, including internal and external drivers, such as changes in the market, technology, and regulatory environment.*

To use scenario planning effectively, organizations must *identify the key drivers that are likely to shape the future of their industry or market,* with a clear **cause-and-effect relationship** between the key drivers and their impacts on organizational operation, business continuity, customers, suppliers, and competitors (Ferguson & Lennox, 2017). The potential impact of each scenario should be analyzed to understand the potential risks and opportunities associated with each scenario and the critical success factors that will determine the organization's **ability to survive** and **thrive** in each scenario (Waldrop & Weber, 2000; Glaesser, 2018).

Scenario planning considers the impact of contingencies on the organization's **financial performance**, **market position**, and **reputation**, as well as its employees, customers, and other stakeholders. This analysis can be conducted using various tools, including *scenario analysis*, *risk analysis*, and *sensitivity analysis*.

Once the potential impacts of each scenario have been analyzed, *plans and actions should be developed to address the potential risks and opportunities.* These plans should be **robust** but **flexible** enough to be implemented in any scenario based on the organization's **objectives** and **priorities**, potential **costs**, **benefits**, and **feasibility** of each plan (Schoemaker, 1995). *The plans should also be communicated effectively throughout the organization to ensure buy-in and support from all stakeholders and **build consensus** and alignment around a **shared vision** of the future* (van der Heijden, 2005; Buchanan & O'Connell, 2006).

Scenario planning can provide several benefits to organizations, including **improved decision-making**, increased **agility** and **flexi-**

bility, and ***better risk management*** (Ramirez, Churchhouse, & Hoffmann, 2018). By anticipating different possible futures, organizations can make more informed decisions and develop contingency plans to prepare for potential risks and opportunities.

Despite the potential benefits of scenario planning, there are also some ***challenges*** associated with this approach. One challenge is the *difficulty of predicting the future with certainty, given the complexity and unpredictability of the business environment*. Secondly, scenario planning requires a high degree of ***creativity and imagination***, as well as the ability to ***think critically*** and ***objectively*** about the future (Glaesser, 2018; Schoemaker, 2008).

Another challenge is the potential for ***bias*** and ***groupthink***, leading to narrow or unrealistic scenarios and plans (Ramirez et al., 2018). Moreover, scenario planning can also be ***time-consuming*** and ***resource-intensive***, requiring a significant investment of time, money, and expertise (Ferguson & Lennox, 2017). This can be a barrier for smaller organizations or those with limited resources. Lastly, scenario planning can be subject to ***cognitive biases*** and errors, such as ***overconfidence, anchoring,*** and ***confirmation bias***, distorting the analysis and decision-making process (Dreyer & Gronhaug, 2014; Ramirez & Wilkinson, 2016).

It is essential to evaluate the impact of cultural and social factors on strategic thinking regularly, using metrics such as ***diversity***, ***inclusion***, and ***innovation***. This can help identify areas for improvement and ensure that strategies effectively address the influence of cultural and social factors on strategic thinking.

In conclusion, strategic thinking is a critical management skill that *allows managers to anticipate and respond to future challenges and opportunities proactively*. It involves taking a **proactive approach** to **decision-making** and **planning**. By developing strategic thinking skills, individuals and organizations can increase their **competitiveness** and **sustainability** and adapt to changing circumstances. By thinking strategically, managers can develop a **long-term plan** that aligns with the organization's vision and goals, creates a sustainable **competitive advantage**, and fosters **innovation** and **creativity**. To develop and apply strategic thinking, managers must cultivate a **growth mindset,** have a deep understanding of their organization's internal and external environment, and communicate effectively with all stakeholders.

Individuals and organizations must prioritize the development of strategic thinking skills to achieve **long-term success**. *Factors such as power distance, individualism versus collectivism, socioeconomic status, education level, and peer influence can shape strategic thinking, leading to different outcomes for organizations* (Harrison & Shirom, 1999; Schmitt & West, 2009). However, these influences can be addressed through strategies such as training and education, diversity and inclusion, open communication and collaboration, and regular evaluation (Goodstein et al., 2014; Robbins & Judge, 2019; Mertens et al., 2017).

Review

1. Strategic thinking is the ability to identify and evaluate long-term opportunities and challenges to create a strategic plan for an organization.

2. Strategic thinking involves evaluating and analyzing data, assessing risks and opportunities, developing a long-term plan, and adapting to changing circumstances.

3. Strategic thinking helps organizations to develop and achieve their long-term goals.

4. Business management involves making decisions that affect the long-term success of an organization.

5. According to Grant (2019), strategic thinking is the process of "formulating objectives, making decisions, and taking actions that determine the long-term performance of an organization" (p. 3).

6. By thinking strategically, managers can identify potential risks and opportunities, develop a plan to mitigate risks and capitalize on opportunities, and ensure that the organization is moving in the right direction.

7. To apply strategic thinking, managers must first define the organization's long-term goals, and then develop a plan that outlines the steps needed to achieve these goals.

8. Strategic thinking is not an innate ability; rather, it is a skill that can be developed and honed over time.

9. To develop strategic thinking skills, managers must cultivate a growth mindset, be open to learning, and continuously seek new information and perspectives.

10. Additionally, managers must have a deep understanding of their organization's vision, mission, values, and goals, as well as its internal and external environment.

CHAPTER 13

ORGANIZATIONAL COMMUNICATION

"The single biggest problem with communication is the illusion that it has taken place."

— George Bernard Shaw

Organizational communication refers to the *process by which individuals and groups exchange information and coordinate their actions.* Effective organizational communication is essential to the successful functioning of any organization as it allows for the sharing of important information, coordination of activities, and creation of a sense of shared purpose among members (Jackson & Rudowski, 2020).

Leaders play a critical role in setting the tone for organizational communication, establishing clear **communication policies**, and **modeling effective communication** practices. They can also encourage a culture of open communication by creating opportunities for **feedback** and actively **seeking employee input**. Research has shown that employees who perceive their leaders as effective communicators are more likely to report higher levels of job satisfaction and organizational commitment.

Formal communication channels are those that are officially recognized by an organization and are used for **official communication**, such as **meetings**, **memoranda**, and **emails**. These channels are used to share official information, make decisions, and provide feedback. Formal communication channels are usually **controlled by the organization** and are used to communicate with employees, customers, and other stakeholders. For example, an organization may use a formal communication channel, such as an email, to provide employees with updates on new policies or organizational changes (Bovee, Thill, & Schatzman, 2016).

Informal communication channels, on the other hand, are not officially recognized by an organization and are used for personal communication. These channels are used to **share personal information**, **build relationships**, and **make contacts**. Informal communication channels are generally not controlled by the organization and include **rumors**, **word-of-mouth**, and **social networks**. For example, an organization may use an informal communication channel, such as a chat room, to allow employees to share personal information and build relationships (Lang, 2018).

Traditional media, such as **print** and **broadcast media**, have been used for many years to communicate with the public. Print media, such as newspapers and magazines, and broadcast media, such as television and radio, are used to share information with a large audience to reach customers and other stakeholders (Kotler, Armstrong, & Saunders, 2018; Jhally, 2006).

One advantage of traditional media, such as print and broadcast media, is their **broad audience reach** and **accessibility**. However, they can also be costly and lack immediacy compared to digital media. Digital media, on the other hand, are more cost-effective and can be accessed quickly by a large audience. However, they can also be **overwhelming** and **unreliable** (Kaplan & Haenlein, 2016; Kates, 2018).

It is impossible to imagine a modern organization that does not utilize digital media. An organization's digital presence is used to share information with a large audience, including customers and other stakeholders. Social media, such as Facebook and Twitter, are used to share information with a large audience and to reach customers. An organization can use traditional and digital media to reach customers and promote a new product (Kaplan & Haenlein, 2016).

When selecting a **communication medium**, it is essential to consider factors such as the **message, audience,** and **desired outcome**. For example, *a sensitive message may be best communicated in person* or through a formal email, while a promotional message may be best communicated through social media or a press release.

To ensure effective communication, organizations should also consider the **preferences and habits of their audience**. For instance, if the target audience is primarily elderly individuals who may not be familiar with digital media, traditional media may be a more effective communication medium (Bovee, Thill, & Schatzman, 2016; Lang, 2018).

While choosing the appropriate communication medium is important, it is equally important to consider the **advantages and disadvantages** of different media and select the **most suitable medium** for a specific **message** and **audience**. Effective communication is critical to the functioning of any organization, and the choice of communication medium plays a significant role in communication effectiveness (Bovee et al., 2016).

A critical aspect of organizational communication is the **coordination process**. This refers to how individuals and groups within an organization work together to achieve common goals. Coordination can be achieved through a variety of means, such as **formal planning**, **negotiation**, and **collaboration**. Effective coordination is essential to the efficient functioning of an organization as it ensures resources are allocated and activities are coordinated consistent with the organization's objectives (Jackson & Rudowski, 2020; Mishra & Mishra, 2019).

A third important aspect of organizational communication — which bears repeating — is creating a **sense of shared purpose** among members. This refers to how **individuals** and **groups identify** and **commit** to the organization's **goals** and **values** and can be achieved through effective communication, as well as by creating opportunities for members to actively **participate in decision-making** and **execution**. Having a sense of shared purpose is essential for **motivating** and **engaging members** of the organization, which increases the organization's effectiveness and performance (Jackson & Rudowski, 2020).

In a study of communication patterns in organizations, Robbins and Judge (2007) found that **satisfaction with communication is positively related to job satisfaction and organizational commitment**. Similarly, another study by Hartog et al. (2004) found that **communication climate**, or the shared perception of communication within an organization, is positively related to job satisfaction and organizational commitment. These studies suggest that effective organizational communication not only **facilitates the exchange of information** and coordination of activities but also contributes to the **well-being** and **commitment** of members of the organization.

Effective communication within an organization also positively affects **organizational performance**. A study by Todorova and Durst (2010) found that organizations with high levels of communication effectiveness had higher levels of organizational performance measured by factors such as **innovation** and **market share**. Effective communication between different departments within an organization positively relates to organizational performance as it leads to more **effective decision-making**.

However, in the fast-paced and technology-driven environment of today, organizations face new challenges when it comes to communicating effectively. Social media and instant messaging platforms, while useful tools for communication, can also lead to *information overload* and *distractions*. In a study by Rosen et al. (2013), employees who frequently use *social media at work* reported *lower levels* of task-focused work and higher levels of *distraction*. Additionally, virtual teams, while offering organizations the ability to tap into a global pool of talent, also present unique communication challenges, such as *time zone differences* and *cultural barriers* (Kirkman, Rosen, & Tesluk, 2004).

These challenges can be addressed by implementing various strategies, such as providing *training* on effective communication, promoting *face-to-face communication*, and establishing clear *guidelines for technology use* in the workplace. In a study conducted by Riggio and Riggio (2008), training programs focusing on communication skills *improved performance*. A study by O'Malley and Tynan (2010) found that organizations that promote face-to-face communication had *higher levels of trust* and *collaboration* among employees.

Communicating clearly and effectively can *boost productivity*, especially since we spend most of our day communicating with others in conversations, emails, meetings, presentations, conference calls, and more. The 7 Cs of communication (Mindtools, n.d.)provide a checklist for constructing clear and effective communication:

1. *Clear.* Be clear about your message's purpose and goal. If you're not clear, your audience won't be either.

2. **Concise.** Stick to the point and keep it brief. Avoid unnecessary sentences and filler words that can make your message needlessly long.

3. **Concrete.** Make sure your message is concrete by providing the necessary details. Use vivid facts and laser-like focus to give a clear picture.

4. **Correct.** Ensure your message is error-free and uses terms that fit your audience's level of knowledge. Check spelling and grammar.

5. **Coherent.** Ensure that your message is logical and that all points are connected and relevant to the main topic. Maintain a consistent tone and flow.

6. **Complete.** Provide your audience with all the information they need to take action.

7. **Courteous.** Keep your communication friendly, open, and honest. Avoid hidden insults or passive-aggressive tones, and keep your reader's viewpoint in mind. Be empathetic to their needs.

In conclusion, effective organizational communication is essential for the successful functioning of any organization. It enables the sharing of important information, coordination of activities, and creating a sense of shared purpose among members. Effective organizational communication also positively affects **organizational performance**, **job satisfaction**, and organizational **commitment**. As organizations face new challenges for effective communication in the technology-driven environment of today, it is important for organizations to implement strategies such as providing communication training, promoting face-to-face communication, and establishing clear guidelines for technology use in the workplace.

Organizations can use **different types** of communication media for **different purposes** and reach **different audiences**. Formal and informal communication channels are used for official and personal communication, respectively. Traditional and digital media are used to share information with a large audience. Effective communication is essential to the functioning of any organization, and the choice of communication media plays a crucial role in communication effectiveness.

Review

1. Organizational communication refers to the process by which individuals and groups exchange information and coordinate their actions.

2. Formal communication channels, such as meetings, memoranda, and emails, are used to share official information and make decisions.

3. A critical aspect of organizational communication is the coordination process, which can be achieved through a variety of

means, such as formal planning, negotiation, and collaboration.

4. A third important aspect of organizational communication is creating a shared purpose among members.

5. Robbins and Judge (2007) found that satisfaction with communication is positively related to job satisfaction and organizational commitment.

6. Todorova and Durst (2010) found that organizations with high levels of communication effectiveness had higher levels of organizational performance, measured by factors such as innovation and market participation.

7. To address these challenges, organizations can implement various strategies, such as providing training on effective communication, and promoting face-to-face communication.

8. Social media and instant messaging platforms, while helpful communication tools, can also cause information overload and distractions.

9. The 7 Cs of communication provide a checklist for constructing clear and effective communication: clear, concise, concrete, correct, coherent, complete, and courteous.

CHAPTER 14

COMMUNICATION AS A BUSINESS STRATEGY

S trategic communication refers to the *process of aligning an organization's communication efforts with its overall goals and objectives.* Effective strategic communication allows managers to **convey their vision**, **goals**, and **expectations** to employees, **resolve conflicts** and **build trust** within the organization (Sriramesh & Vercic, 2003; Lencioni, 2002).

Effective communication is essential for successful management and organizational performance.

Strategic communication enables managers to align their communication efforts with the organization's goals and objectives. It also enables managers to provide ***feedback*** and ***guidance***, ***resolve conflicts*** and ***build trust*** with members. Additionally, effective communication is key to fostering a ***positive*** and ***productive*** work environment, as well as facilitating ***collaboration*** and ***teamwork*** (Barkhuizen & Bosch, 2016; Covey, 1989). This can improve employee engagement, motivation, and productivity and foster a positive and productive work environment. Strategic communication also p*lays a fundamental role in building and maintaining relationships with stakeholders.* Managers can use strategic communication to ***build trust*** and ***credibility*** with stakeholders and manage their expectations and perceptions. This can improve the organization's reputation and enhance its ability to obtain funding and support from stakeholders.

Active listening is essential for developing strategic communication in management. Active listening *involves fully focusing on the speaker and trying to understand their message rather than waiting for an opportunity to respond.* This can be achieved by paying attention to ***nonverbal signals***, asking ***clarifying questions***, and ***summarizing*** the speaker's message. Active listening can improve communication by reducing misunderstandings and fostering a more inclusive and collaborative work environment (Barkhuizen & Bosch, 2016).

Managers should be ***clear*** and ***specific*** in their communication, ***avoiding jargon*** and ***technical terms*** that may confuse employees. They should also consider the ***tone*** and ***level of formality***, as this can have a significant impact on how the message is received. *Clear and concise communication can improve understanding and reduce confusion, which can help managers achieve their goals more effectively* (Lencioni, 2002).

Managers can improve their communication skills by *being aware of their own communication styles and making the necessary adjustments*. Some managers may be **too direct** or **assertive**, while others may be more passive or indirect. By being aware of these tendencies and making adjustments, managers can become more effective communicators.

Managers can also use various communication tools to improve their strategic communication skills. These may include email, instant messaging, video conferencing, and social media. These tools can be used to communicate with employees as well as other managers and stakeholders within the organization. They can also help **increase efficiency** and **productivity** by reducing the need for face-to-face meetings and travel (Sriramesh & Vercic, 2003). However, managers must be aware of the possible drawbacks of these tools, such as the potential for misinterpretation or lack of personal connection.

In summary, developing strategic communication in management is essential to achieving organizational goals and building positive relationships with stakeholders. Managers can improve their communication skills by using techniques such as **active listening**, clear and **concise communication**, and awareness of communication *style*. They can also use various communication tools to increase efficiency and productivity.

By taking the time to develop their strategic communication skills, managers can become more effective leaders and contribute to the overall success of the organization.

Review

1. Strategic planning refers to the process of aligning an organization's communication efforts with its overall goals and objectives.

2. Effective communication is essential for successful management and organizational leadership.

3. Strategic communication enables managers to provide feedback and guidance, as well as resolve conflicts and foster collaboration with team members.

4. Effective communication is key to developing a positive organizational culture, promoting motivation, and improving decision-making.

5. Strategic communication includes internal and external communication and is essential for creating a brand image and building strong relationships with stakeholders.

Part IV: Discussion Questions

1. What is the importance of organizational communication for the functioning of an organization?

2. What are the formal and informal channels of organizational communication, and how are they important for communication effectiveness?

3. What is the coordination process in organizational communication, and why is it essential for organizational efficiency?

4. How can a sense of shared purpose be created among members of an organization through communication?

5. How does organizational communication affect employee job satisfaction and commitment?

6. What role does the communication climate play in employee job satisfaction and commitment?

7. What studies have shown the relationship between organizational communication and employee job satisfaction and commitment?

8. What are the different types of communication media used by organizations?

9. What are formal communication channels, and how are they used in an organization?

10. How do informal communication channels differ from formal ones?

11. What role do traditional media play in an organization's communication?

12. How do digital media affect communication in an organization?

13. What factors should be considered when choosing communication media for an organization?

14. What are the advantages and disadvantages of using different communication media in an organization?

15. How does the choice of communication media affect communication effectiveness in an organization?

16. What role does communication play in the functioning of an organization, and how can communication effectiveness be improved?

17. How can different communication media be combined to achieve effective organizational communication?

18. What is the importance of strategic communication in managing an organization?

19. How can strategic communication improve organizational performance and work environment?

20. How can active listening help improve strategic communication?

21. What is important to consider when communicating clearly and concisely in a work environment?

22. How can managers improve their communication skills?

23. How can strategic communication influence the building and maintenance of relationships with stakeholders?

24. How can clear and specific communication influence under-standing and reduce conflicts in the workplace?

25. How can tone and formality in communication influence how the message is received?

26. What is strategic thinking, and why is it essential for managers in today's business environment?

27. How does strategic thinking help organizations achieve their long-term goals and increase their competitiveness and sustain-ability?

28. What are some of the strategies that managers can use to apply strategic thinking in their decision-making and planning pro-cesses?

29. How can individuals and organizations develop their strategic thinking skills?

30. What is data analytics, and how can it help businesses to gain a better understanding of their customers, competitors, and the market?

31. What is the cultural dimensions theory developed by Hofstede, and how can cultural factors influence strategic thinking?

32. How can social factors such as socioeconomic status, education level, and peer influence impact strategic thinking?

33. What are some benefits of fostering a culture of innovation, risk-taking, and continuous learning in organizations?

34. How can strategic thinking foster innovation and creativity in organizations?

35. What are some of the challenges that managers may face when trying to apply strategic thinking in their decision-making and planning processes?

36. What is scenario planning, and how can it be beneficial for organizations?

37. How does scenario planning differ from traditional strategic planning methods?

38. What are the steps involved in scenario planning?

39. What are the key drivers that organizations must identify to use scenario planning effectively?

40. What are the potential impacts that organizations should analyze for each scenario in scenario planning?

41. What are some tools that organizations can use to analyze potential impacts in scenario planning?

42. How should organizations develop plans and actions in scenario planning?

43. What are the potential benefits of scenario planning for organizations?

44. What are some challenges associated with scenario planning?

45. How can organizations evaluate the impact of cultural and social factors on strategic thinking?

BIBLIOGRAPHY

Achor, S. & Peterson, E. (2008). *Bringing the science of positive psychology to life.* Aspirant.

Achor, S. (2010). *The happiness advantage.* Crown Business.

Amabile, T. & Kramer, S. (2011). *The progress principle: Using small wins to ignite joy, engagement, and creativity at work.* Harvard Business School Press.

Amabile, T. M. (1988). A model of creativity and innovation in organizations. *Research in Organizational Behavior*, 10, 123–167.

Amabile, T. M. (1998). How to kill creativity. *Harvard Business Review*, 76(5), 76–87.

American Psychological Association. (2017). *Stress.* Retrieved from https://www.apa.org/helpcenter/stress.

Bar-On, R. (1997). *The emotional intelligence inventory (EQ-I): Technical manual.* Multi-Health Systems.

Barkhuizen, N., & Bosch, A. (2016). The role of communication in the management of change. *Journal of Change Management*, 16(2), 159–174.

Barkhuizen, N., & Bosch, A. (2016). The role of effective communication in the management of organizations. *Journal of Applied Management and Entrepreneurship*, 21(2), 1–9.

Barrick, M. R., & Mount, M. K. (1991). The big five personality dimensions and job performance: A meta-analysis. *Personnel Psychology*, 44(1), 1–26.

Bass, B. M. (1985). (1990). *Bass & Stogdill's Handbook of Leadership: Theory, Research, and Managerial Applications (3rd Ed.)*. Free Press.

Bass, B. M. (1985). *Leadership and performance beyond expectations*. Free Press.

Beck, A. T. (2011). Terapia cognitiva: Fundamentos y aplicaciones. Madrid: Editorial Médica Panamericana.

Bennis, W. & Goldsmith, J. (2005). *Learning to lead: a workbook on becoming a leader*. Basic Books.

Bhattacharya, C.B., Sen, S. & Korschun, D. (2008). Using corporate social responsibility to win the war for talent. *MIT Sloan Management Review*, 49(2), 37-44.

Blanchard, K. H., & Johnson, S. (1982). *The one minute manager*. William Morrow.

Bovee, C. L., Thill, J. V., & Schatzman, L. (2016). *Business communication today (13th Ed.)*. Pearson.

Boyatzis, R. E., Smith, M. L., & Blaize, N. (2006). Developing sustainable leaders through coaching and compassion. *Academy of Management Learning & Education*, 5(1), 8–24.

Boyd, J., & Myers, D. G. (2011). *The meaning of the scores on personality tests: A guide for the development and use of the Myers-Briggs Type Indicator*. Consulting Psychologists Press.

Bramson, R. M., & Glasser, R. (2017). *I Hear You: Repair Communication Breakdowns, Negotiate Successfully, and Build Consensus … In Three Simple Steps.* AMACOM.

Bramson, R. M., & Glasser, S. B. (2017). *Mediation: a practical guide for resolving disputes.* American Bar Association.

Brown, B. (2018). *Dare to lead: brave work, tough conversations.* Random House.

Brown, K. W., & Ryan, R. M. (2003). The benefits of being present: Mindfulness and its role in psychological well-being. *Journal of Personality and Social Psychology,* 84(4), 822–848.

Brown, M. E., & Treviño, L. K. (2006). Ethical leadership: A review and future directions. *The Leadership Quarterly,* 17(6), 595–616.

Brown, S.L., Nesse, R.M., Vinkur, A.D., & Smith, D.M. (2003). Providing social support may be more beneficial than receiving it: Results from a prospective study of mortality. *Psychological Science,* 14(4), 320-327.

Buchanan, S., & O'Connell, A. (2006). *A brief history of scenario planning.* In *S. Ramírez (Ed.), Business planning for turbulent times: New methods for applying scenarios* (pp. 17–32). Earthscan.

Buckingham, M. & Clifton, D.O. (2001). *Now, discover your strengths.* Free.

Buckingham, M., & Coffman, C. (1999). *First, break all the rules: what the world's greatest managers do differently.* Simon & Schuster.

Burke, W. W. (2008). *Organization change: Theory and practice.* Sage.

Cabrera, E. (20120). The six essentials of workplace positivity. *People & Strategy* 35/1 (2012), 50–60.

Cameron, E. & Green, M. (2015). *making sense of change management: a complete guide to the models, tools and techniques of organizational change.* Kogan Page.

Cameron, K. S., & Quinn, R. E. (2006). *Diagnosing and changing organizational culture: Based on the competing values framework.* John Wiley & Sons.

Carmeli, A., & Josman, N. (2008). The relationship between emotional intelligence and work attitudes, behavior and outcomes: an examination among senior managers. *Journal of Managerial Psychology,* 23(8), 888–905.

Cascio, W.F. (2003). Changes in workers, work, and organizations. In W. Borman, R. Klimoski, & D. Ilgen (Eds.), *Handbook of psychology.* Volume 12: *Industrial and organizational psychology.* Wiley.

Chalofsky, N.E. (2010). *Meaningful workplaces: Reframing how and where we work.* Jossey-Bass.

Chattu, V. K., Yaya, S., and Sahu, P. K. (2020). Sleep Disorders in the Context of COVID-19 Pandemic: A Review of a New Emerging Literature. *Journal of Neurology Research,* 10(2), 55–69.

Christensen, C. M. (1997). The innovator's dilemma: When new technologies cause great firms to fail. Harvard Business Review Press.

Costa, P. T., & McCrae, R. R. (1992). Four ways five factors are basic. *Personality and individual differences,* 13(6), 653–665.

Costa, P. T., & McCrae, R. R. (1992). Professional manual revised NEO personality inventory (NEO-PI-R) and NEO five-factor inventory (NEO-FFI). *Psychological Assessment Resources.*

Covey, S. (1989). *The 7 habits of highly effective people: powerful lessons in personal change.* Simon and Schuster.

Cropley, A. J. (2006). In praise of convergent thinking. *Scientific American,* 295(3), 84–91.

Csikszentmihalyi, M. (1990). *Flow: The psychology of optimal experience.* Harper & Row.

Danner, D.D., Snowdon, D.A., & Friesen, W.V. (2001). Positive emotions in early life and longevity: Findings from the nun study. *Journal of Personality and Social Psychology*, 80, 804-813.

Day, D. V., Fleenor, J. W., Atwater, L. E., Sturm, R. E., & McKee, R. A. (2014). Advances in leader and leadership development: A review of 25 years of research and theory. *The Leadership Quarterly*, 25(1), 63–82.

De Dreu, C. K., & Weingart, L. R. (2003). *Collaborative and cooperative intergroup relations.* In P. J. Carroll (Ed.), *Handbook of Industrial, Work and Organizational Psychology* (pp. 255–296). Sage.

De Dreu, C. K., & Weingart, L. R. (2003b). Task versus relationship conflict, team performance, and team member satisfaction: A meta-analysis. *Journal of Applied Psychology*, 88(4), 741–749.

Deci, E. L., & Ryan, R. M. (2000). The "what" and "why" of goal pursuits: Human needs and the self-determination of behavior. *Psychological Inquiry*, 11(4), 227–268.

Deci, E. L., Koestner, R., & Ryan, R. M. (1999). A meta-analytic review of experiments examining the effects of extrinsic rewards on intrinsic motivation. *Psychological Bulletin*, 125(6), 627–668.

Den Hartog, & Kompier, M. (1999). The relationship between leadership and employees' well-being. *Journal of Occupational Health Psychology*, 4(4), 350–360.

Den Hartog, D. N., Koopman, P. L., & Thierry, H. (1999). Leadership and organizational culture: The leader-culture connection in five Dutch organizations. *The Leadership Quarterly*, 10(2), 103–128.

Den Hartog, D. N., Koopman, P. L., Thierry, H., & Verburg, R. M. (2004). The relationship between communication climate and communication satisfaction: The impact of organizational change. *Journal of Occupational Health Psychology*, 9(1), 67–79.

Den Hartog, Koopman, P. L. (Eds.). (2016). *Organizational communication and organizational development: Exploring the cross-vergence*. Routledge.

Diener, E., Nickerson, C., Lucas, R.E., & Sandvik, E. (2002). Dispositional affect and job outcomes. *Social Indicators Research*, 59, 229-259.

DiTomasso, N. A., & Spiegler, M. D. (2011). Efficacy of cognitive therapy in the treatment of psychological disorders: A systematic review of the literature. *Journal of Psychotherapy*, 22(2), 19–37.

Dreyer, H. C., & Gronhaug, K. (2014). The advantages and limitations of scenario approaches for strategic foresight. *European Journal of Futures Research*, 2(1), 1–13.

DuFrene, D. D., & Toth, E. L. (2016). *Organizational communication for survival: Making work, work*. Routledge.

Duggan, J. (2016). *Conflict resolution: how to communicate effectively and resolve conflict in your relationship*. Penguin Random House.

Dutton, J.E. (2003). *Energize your workplace: How to create and sustain high-quality connections at work*. Jossey-Bass.

Dweck, C. S. (2006). *Mindset: The new psychology of success. Random House*.

Ferguson, R., & Lennox, J. (2017). Scenario planning and strategic foresight. *Strategy & Leadership*, 45(6), 33–39.

Ferris, G. R., Frink, D. D., Galang, M. C., & Kacmar, C. J. (Eds.). (2016). *Research in personnel and human resources management.* Emerald Group.

Fischer, A. H., & Manstead, A. S. (2000). *The relation between gender and emotions in different cultures.* In A. Fischer (Ed.), *Gender and emotion: Social psychological perspectives* (pp. 71–94). Cambridge University Press.

Fossum, M. A., & Mason, D. S. (1986). *When talk works: profiles of mediators.* Jossey-Bass.

Fredrickson, B.L. (2009*). Positivity.* Crown.

Fredrickson, B.L. & Branigan, C. (2005). Positive emotions broaden the scope of attention and thought-action repertoires. *Cognition and Emotion,* 19, 313-332.

Furnham, A., (2006). *The psychology of behaviour at work: the individual in the organization.* Routledge.

Furr, Nathan and Jeffrey H. Dyer. Leading your team into the unknown. *Harvard Business Review* (Dec 2014): 1–10.

Gardner, H. (1983). *Frames of mind: the theory of multiple intelligences.* Basic Books.

Gardner, W. L., & Avolio, B. J. (1998). The charismatic relationship: a dramaturgical perspective. *The Leadership Quarterly,* 9(4), 43–62.

Glaesser, D. (2018). Scenario planning: A review. *Journal of Contingencies and Crisis Management,* 26(2), 235–246.

Goleman, D. (1998). *Working with Emotional Intelligence.* Bantam Books.

Goleman, D. (2001). An I.E.-based theory of performance. In C. Cherniss & D. Goleman (Eds.), *The emotionally intelligent workplace: How to select for, measure, and improve emotional intelligence in individuals, groups, and organizations* (pp. 27–44). Jossey-Bass.

Goleman, D. (2006). *Emotional intelligence: Why it can matter more than IQ*. Bloomsbury.

Goleman, D., Boyatzis, R. E., & McKee, A. (2002). *Primal leadership: Realizing the power of emotional intelligence*. Harvard Business Review Press.

Goodstein, L. D., Nolan, T. M., & Pfeiffer, J. W. (2014). *Applied strategic planning: An introduction. Society for Human Resource Management.*

Gottman, J. M . (1999). *The seven principles for making marriage work: a practical guide from the country's foremost relationship expert*. Crown Publishers.

Gottman, J. M. (2016). *The science of trust: emotional attunement for couples*. W. W. Norton.

Grant, A.M. (2008). The significance of task significance: Job performance effects, relational mechanisms, and boundary conditions. *Journal of Applied Psychology*, 93(1), 108-124.

Grant, R. M. (2019). *Contemporary strategy analysis: text and cases edition (10th ed.)*. Wiley-Blackwell.

Groysberg, B., Lee, L., & Nohria, N. (2008). The new path to the C-suite. *Harvard Business Review*, 86(10), 60–70.

Gudykunst, W. B. (2003). *Cross-cultural and intercultural communication*. Sage.

Gustafsson, A. (2017). The Impact of employee relationships on team performance. *Journal of Business and Management*, 15(2), 1–10.

Harrison, S. H., & Shirom, A. (1999). *Organizational diagnosis and assessment: Bridging theory and practice.* Sage.

Hart, R. (2019). Communication skills in conflict resolution. In R. J. R. Levesque (Ed.), Encyclopedia of Adolescence (pp. 1–10). Springer International.

Harter, J.K., Schmidt, F., & Hayes, B. (2002). Business-unit-level relationship between employee satisfaction, employee engagement, and business outcomes: A meta-analysis. *Journal of Applied Psychology, 87,* 268-279.

Hess, T., & Bacouel-Jentjens, S. (2018). Strategic thinking with data analytics: What's in it for decision makers? *Journal of Business Research, 89,* 256–265.

Hill, L.A. & Lineback, K. (2011). *Being the boss: The three imperatives for becoming a great leader.* Harvard Business Press.

Hitt, M. A., Ireland, R. D., & Hoskisson, R. E. (2017). Strategic management: Concepts and cases: Competitiveness and globalization. Cengage.

Hoegl, M., & Gemuenden, H. G. (2001). Teamwork quality and the success of innovative projects: A theoretical concept and empirical evidence. *Organization Science, 12*(4), 435–449.

Hofstede, G. (1980). *Culture's consequences: International differences in work-related values.* Sage.

Hofstede, G. (2011). Dimensionalizing Cultures: The Hofstede Model in Context. Online *Readings in Psychology and Culture, 2*(1).

Hu, J, Liden, R. C., & Wu, J. (2011). The effects of leader and follower self-awareness on accuracy of leadership self-ratings and performance. *Personnel Psychology, 64*(2), 393–430.

Ireland, R. D., & Hitt, M. A. (2005). Achieving and maintaining strategic competitiveness in the 21st century: The role of strategic leadership. *Academy of Management Executive,* 19(4), 63–77.

Isen, A.M., Rosenzweig, A.S., & Young, M.J. (1991). The influence of positive affect on clinical problem solving. *Medical Decision Making*, 11, 221-227.

Jackson, S. & Rudowski, J. (2020). *Organizational communication: theories and practices*. Routledge.

Jhally, S. (2006). *The spectacle of accumulation: Essays in culture, media, and politics*. Peter Lang.

Kaplan, A. M., & Haenlein, M. (2016). Business models for strategic social media management. *Business horizons*, 59(4), 417–426.

Kates, A. (2018). The role of the Internet in business communication. *Journal of Business Communication*, 55(1), 3–23.

Kendall, E. (2010). Stress management techniques. *American Family Physician*, 82(7), 675–682.

Kerns, C. D., & Barclay, E. (2011). Promoting ethical behavior and organizational citizenship behaviors: The influence of corporate ethical values. *Journal of Business Ethics*, 98(4), 635–647.

Kirkman, B. L., Rosen, B., & Tesluk, P. E. (2004). The impact of cultural diversity on team processes and outcomes. *International Journal of Cross Cultural Management*, 4(2), 143–168.

Kirschenbaum, D. (1984). Self-regulation and sport psychology: Nurturing and emerging symbiosis. *Journal of Sport Psychology*, 6(2), 159-183.

Kotler, P., Armstrong, G., & Saunders, J. (2018). *Principles of marketing (15th ed.)*. Pearson.

Kotter, J. P. (1996). *Leading change*. Harvard Business Review Press.

Kouzes, J. M., & Posner, B. Z. (2007). *The leadership challenge.* John Wiley & Sons.

Kozlowski, S. W., & Ilgen, D. R. (2006). Enhancing the effectiveness of work groups and teams. *Psychological science in the public interest,* 7(3), 77–124.

Kroenke, K., Spitzer, R. L., & Williams, J. B. (2007). The PHQ-9: validity of a brief depression severity measure. *Journal of General Internal Medicine,* 22(2), 165–172.

Krogh, J., Nordentoft, M., & Sterne, J. A. (2017). Exercise for depression. *Cochrane Database of Systematic Reviews* (9).

Kwok, L. C., & Wang, D. (2018). The impact of delegation on organizational performance: a meta-analysis. *Journal of Business Research,* 84, 199–208.

Kwok, O. M., & Wang, L. (2018). The role of communication in conflict management: A systematic review. *Journal of Communication Management,* 22(2), 169–184.

Kwok, Y. Y., & Wang, D. (2018). Conflict management in the workplace: a review of the literature. *Journal of Business and Technical Communication,* 32(4), 393–428.

Lam, D. W. (2017). Developing self-awareness in counseling and psychotherapy. In C. E. Watkins Jr., & D. L. Milne (Eds.), *The Wiley International Handbook of Clinical Supervision* (pp. 289–312). Wiley-Blackwell.

Lang, D. (2018). *Informal communication in organizations: Form, function, and technology.* Routledge.

Lencioni, P. (2002). *The five dysfunctions of a team: a leadership fable.* Jossey-Bass.

Locke, E. A., & Latham, G. P. (2002). Building a practically useful theory of goal setting and task motivation: A 35-year odyssey. *American Psychologist,* 57(9), 705–717.

Lopes, P. N., Brackett, M. A., Nezlek, J. B., Schütz, A., Sellin, I., & Salovey, P. (2004). Emotional intelligence and social interaction. *Personality and Social Psychology Review*, 8(3), 228–255.

Lopes, P. N., Côté, S., & Miners, C. T. (2006). Emotional intelligence, personality, and the perceived quality of social relationships. *Personality and individual differences*, 40(8), 1603–1613.

Luthans, F., & Peterson, S. J. (2002). Employee engagement and manager self-efficacy. *Journal of Management Development*, 21(5), 376–387.

Luthans, F., Avolio, B. J., Avey, J. B., & Norman, S. M. (2007). Positive psychological capital: Measurement and relationship with performance and satisfaction. *Personnel Psychology*, 60(3), 541–572.

Lyubomirsky, S. (2007). *The how of happiness: A scientific approach to getting the life you want.* The Penguin Press.

Lyubomirsky, S., King, L., & Diener, E. (2005). The benefits of frequent positive affect: Does happiness lead to success? *Psychological Bulletin*, 131(6), 803-855.

Mainiero, L.A. & Sullivan, S.E. (2006). *The opt-out revolt: why people are leaving companies to create kaleidoscope careers.* Davies-Black.

Mathe, H., & Scott-Ladd, B. (2016). Developing strategic thinking through an inclusive approach to strategy. *Journal of Management Development*, 35(6), 727–740.

Matsumoto, D., Yoo, S. H., & Fontaine, J. (2008). Mapping expressive differences around the world: The relationship between emotional display rules and individualism versus collectivism. *Journal of Cross-Cultural Psychology*, 39(1), 55–74.

Mertens, W., Recker, J., Kohlborn, T., & Kummer, T. F. (2017). Data science and big data analytics: what are the challenges for research in information systems? *Journal of Business and Information Systems Engineering,* 59(4), 259–269.

Mindtools. "The 7 Cs of Communication: A Checklist for Clear Communication".

Mintzberg, H. (1994). The rise and fall of strategic planning: Reconceiving roles for planning, plans, planners. Simon and Schuster.

Mishra, A. & Mishra, S. (2019). *Organizational communication: concepts, contexts, and applications.* Sage.

Mor Barak, M. E., Cherin, D. A., & Berkman, S. (1998). Organizational and personal dimensions in diversity climate: Ethnic and gender differences in employee perceptions. *Journal of Applied Behavioral Science,* 34(1), 82–104.

Morsy, L. A. (2017). *Organizational communication: Strategies and skills.* Routledge.

Northouse, P. G. (2016). *Leadership: theory and practice* (7th ed.). Sage.

O'Malley, L., & Tynan, R. (2010). The impact of face-to-face communication on trust and collaboration in virtual teams. *Journal of Computer-Mediated Communication,* 15(4), 1–20.

Pearson, C. & Porath, C. (2009). *The cost of bad behavior: How incivility is damaging your business and what to do about it.* Penguin Group.

Pink, D. H. (2009). *Drive: the surprising truth about what motivates us.* Penguin.

Ramirez, R., Churchhouse, S., & Hoffmann, J. (2018). A new tool for scenario planning in highly uncertain environments: The dynamic scenario builder. *Futures,* 100, 17–28.

Rath, T. & Clifton, D.O. (2005). *How full is your bucket?* Gallup.

Richards, J. (2017). The importance of positive relationships for mental health. *Journal of Mental Health and Wellness*, 2(1), 1–5.

Riggio, R. E. (2009). Escuchar la retroalimentación: el papel de la personalidad y la capacidad cognitiva. *Revista de Psicología Aplicada*, 94(1), 114–121.

Riggio, R. E. (2017). The relationship between empathy and stress in the workplace. *Journal of Organizational Behavior*, 38(1), 1–15.

Riggio, R. E., Riggio, H. R. (2008). Listening and communication training: a meta-analysis. *Journal of Applied Psychology*, 93(4), 951–957.

Rink, F. A., Harvey, M., & Thompson, M. (2017). The influence of diversity on strategic thinking quality: An empirical study. *International Journal of Management*, 34(1), 27–40.

Robbins, S. P., & Judge, T. A (2017). *Organizational behavior* (17th ed.). Pearson.

Robbins, S. P., & Judge, T. A. (2019). *Essentials of organizational behavior (14th ed.).* Pearson.

Roberts, L.M., Spreitzer, G., Dutton, J., Quinn, R., Heaphy, E., & Barker, B. (2005, January). Play to your strengths. *Harvard Business Review*, 75-80.

Rohrbeck, R., Battistella, C., & Huizingh, E. (2013). Corporate foresight: An emerging field with a rich tradition. *Technological Forecasting and Social Change,* 80(4), 595–601.

Rosen, L. D., Carrier, L., Cheever, N. A., & Rokkum, J. (2013). The effects of instant messaging on work-related communication: an experimental study. *Computers in Human Behavior*, 29(1), 87–94.

Ryan, M. K., Arnold, J. A., & Tindall, K. (2015). Work group diversity and group performance: An integrative model and research agenda. *Journal of Applied Psychology,* 100(2), 265–276.

Saks, A. M. (2006). Antecedents and consequences of employee engagement. *Journal of Managerial Psychology*, 21(7), 600–619.

Salovey, P. & Mayer, J. D. (1990). Emotional intelligence. *Imagination, cognition and personality,* 9(3), 185–211.

Sanders, T. (2011). *Today we are rich: Harnessing the power of total confidence.* Tyndale House.

Schermerhorn, J. R., Hunt, J. G., & Osborn, R. N. (2017). *Organizational behavior.* John Wiley & Sons.

Schmitt, N., & West, M. A. (2009). *Handbook of organizational behavior* (2nd ed.). Wiley-Blackwell.

Schoemaker, P. J. (1995). Scenario planning: A tool for strategic thinking. *Sloan Management Review,* 36(2), 25–40.

Schoemaker, P. J. (2008). The future of scenarios: Challenges and opportunities. In G. Wright & R. Goodwin (Eds.), *Decision making and planning under uncertainty: Proceedings of the 10th International Conference on Decision Making and Decision Support Systems in Service of Sustainable Development* (pp. 79–94). Kluwer Academic.

Schutte, N. S., Malouff, J. M., Thorsteinsson, E. B., Bhullar, N., & Rooke, S. E. (2007). A meta-analytic investigation of the relationship between emotional intelligence and health. *Personality and Individual Differences*, 42(6), 921–933.

Schwenk, C. R. (1984). Cognitive simplification processes in strategic decision-making. *Strategic Management Journal,* 5(2), 111–128.

Scott, L., & Kostere, K. (2018). *Organizational communication: a critical approach*. Routledge.

Seligman, M.E.P. (2002). *Authentic happiness*. Free.

Senge, P. (1990). *The fifth discipline: the art & practice of the learning organization*. Doubleday.

Sisodia, R.S., Wolfe, D.B., & Sheth, J.N. (2007). *Firms of endearment*. Wharton School.

Sosik, J. J., & Megerian, L. E. (2014). Understanding leader emotional intelligence and performance: The role of self-other agreement on transformational leadership perceptions. *Group & Organization Management*, 39(5), 555–576.

Sriramesh, K., & Vercic, D. (2003). *The global public relations handbook: Theory, research, and practice*. Routledge.

Staw, B., Sutton, R., & Pelled, L. (1994). Employee positive emotion and favorable outcomes at the workplace. *Organization Science*, 5, 51-71.

Staw, B.M. & Barsade, S.G. (1993). Affect and managerial performance: A test of the sadder-but-wiser vs. happier-and-smarter hypothesis. *Administrative Science Quarterly*, 38, 304-331.

Strock, J.M. (2010). *Serve to lead*. STL Press.

Tenbrunsel, A. E., & Smith-Crowe, K. (2008). Ethical decision making: Where we've been and where we're going. *Academy of Management Annals*, 2(1), 545–607.

Triandis, H. C. (1994). *Culture and Social Behavior*. McGraw-Hill.

Ulrich, D. & Ulrich, W. (2010). *The why of work*. McGraw Hill.

van der Heijden, K. (1996). *Scenarios: The art of strategic conversation*. John Wiley & Sons.

van der Heijden, K. (2005). Scenarios and forecasting: Two perspectives. *Technological Forecasting and Social Change*, 72(6), 761–767.

Voegtlin, C., & Greenwood, M. (2016). *Corporate social responsibility and human rights in Asia: Developing sustainable and responsible business strategies.* Routledge.

Waldrop, M. M., & Weber, L. J. (2000). Strategies of the largest and smallest firms in a mature industry: A scenario planning approach. *Long Range Planning, 33*(2), 272–294.

Wrzesniewski, A., McCauley, C.R., Rozin, P., & Schwartz, B. (1997). Jobs, careers, and callings: People's relations to their work. *Journal of Research in Personality*, 31, 21-33.

www.ingramcontent.com/pod-product-compliance
Lightning Source LLC
Chambersburg PA
CBHW070340220526
45467CB00001B/188